# English
# Traditional
# Customs

# English Traditional Customs
## Christina Hole

*Drawings by Gay John Galsworthy*

Rowman and Littlefield
Totowa, New Jersey

First published in the United States 1975
by Rowman and Littlefield, Totowa, N.J.

© Christina Hole 1975

Library of Congress Cataloging in Publication Data

Hole, Christina.
English traditional customs

Previous editions published under title: English customs & usage.
1. England—Social life and customs. 1. Title.
DA110.H597 1975          394'.0942          75-14365
ISBN 0–87471–736–1

Printed in Great Britain by
Bristol Typesetting Co. Ltd, Bristol

# Contents

# Contents

# Preface

*English Custom and Usage* was first written a little over forty years ago, and was published in the early years of the second Great War of this century. This book was intended to provide a, necessarily, short account of some of the more interesting traditional customs and ceremonies of England, as these existed at that time, and some of those which had only recently lapsed. Of the former, there were then, and still are, a great many, for the English as a whole are great lovers of old ways and very tenacious in habit. Some of the customs that still flourish today are very old indeed, and are rooted in ancient pagan belief and practice, like the Furry Dance at Helston, or the vigorous Haxey Hood Game. Many are medieval in origin, like most of those associated with our long-established fairs, or the Tichborne Dole, which dates from the twelfth century, or the Wyfold Rose, or Lichfield's Greenhill Bower. Others again are comparatively new, but have already become firmly traditional. Curious wills and charities of different periods have provided some of these, from the late seventeenth-century Maids Money at Guildford, for which the competitors must throw dice, to the elaborate Knillian ceremony which takes place once every five years by Knill's Steeple on the top of Worvas Hill, at St Ives in Cornwall, and has done regularly since 1801. Younger still, but seemingly already well rooted amongst our fixed customs are the Christmas cards which first appeared in 1843, and quite modern customs like the Oranges and Lemons ceremony at St Clement Danes, or the sad little Lilies and Roses ceremony held in memory of King Henry VI in the Tower of London, both of which came into being during the present century.

These customs, and much else of the same sort, were described in the first *English Custom and Usage*. Now, however, the time has come when the book must be re-written. *English Traditional Customs* has replaced it. In the interval between the two books there have been many changes. Some have been caused by natural wastage. Ideas alter. Once popular customs, like the giving of Valentine cards and gifts, fall into disfavour for no particular reason. The two wars of our period necessarily stopped for the time being all the traditional ceremonies which involved bonfires by night, or fireworks, and some of these were not afterwards restored, though most of them were. Odd local reasons have occasionally accounted for the loss of local customs, as in one Oxfordshire village where the performance of an ancient and very interesting Mumming Play ceased because the wife of the chief actor, who kept the properties, destroyed the masks in a fit of spring-cleaning fervour, and no one could thereafter be found who had the energy, or perhaps the skill, to make a new set. Motor-roads tearing their untramelled way across traditional festival grounds, or new housing following the path of shifting populations over similar territory, have often swept away, or at least moved to a less happy site, the customary games or dances, or the unofficial fairs that used to take place there. And hooliganism, that bugbear of the last few years, has not infrequently done its best – or worst – to hasten on the decline of some age-old and lively customs. At Sherborne, for instance, Pack Monday Fair has been ushered in for the past five hundred years or so by the appearance at dawn of a cheerful and noisy gathering of young people, known as Teddy Rowe's Band. The racket they made woke everybody up, but people put up with it all for the sake of the old tradition. But in 1964, the police were forced by the intrusion of hooligans to ban the parade for that year, and to renew the ban annually ever since.

Not all the changes of the last forty years have been in the direction of decline. Folk-custom is tough and lingers a long time in the communal memory; quite often it starts up again in a particular district when least expected, after being allowed to lapse for many years. In 1948, the Pancake Race at Olney was revived, after being abandoned during the War, and it has continued annually ever since. This race is said to have started in Olney in 1445, and to have been run there intermittently thereafter, with only occasional interruptions of varying lengths. Now it runs again regularly in its old home, and has been imitated in various other places, including, since 1950, the town of Liberal, in Kansas, USA. At Wishford Magna in Wiltshire, also, an old part of the Grovely custom has been restored. Here, certain ceremonies have to be observed annually on 29 May, in order to maintain the villagers' wood-gathering rights in Grovely Forest. Formerly, one of these ceremonies was the visit of four women carrying oak-sprigs, and some other representatives of the village, to Salisbury during the course of the day, where first they danced before the Cathedral, and then entered the building to assert their rights. This continued until the beginning of the nineteenth century, when both dance and claim were transferred to the front of the rectory at Wishford. But, in 1951, the old ceremony was restored, and the ancient claim is once more made in the central Church of the diocese, as it used to be for centuries before.

Most long-established customs ought to be celebrated on a particular date, and in theory, most of them still are. But it is not always possible to be certain, as it used to be, that an event will fall on the precise day, and not on the nearest Saturday or, if there is one handy, on the nearest Bank Holiday. This, of course, is a matter of local convenience, which makes it very difficult to draw up anything like a Calendar of Folk Customs. A still further modern complication is caused by the new Spring and Autumn Holidays, anniversaries which, unlike the folk-holidays, have no real meaning of their own, but do inevitably draw the older celebrations into their orbit. This is perhaps not very important, except that anything which tends to weaken an old custom's association with its beginnings is a pity, and moreover, it is confusing. What really is important is that so many of our old traditional ways do remain with us, with all that they mean of light and colour and old memory; and that notwithstanding the steady pressures of an industrial age, and every sort of change and difficulty, most of them seem likely to go on doing so for a long while yet to come.

CHRISTINA HOLE

# 1 The Christmas Season

ON CHRISTMAS DAY, that most dearly loved of all Christian festivals, the Church celebrates the Birthday of Our Lord, even though no one knows exactly on what day He was born. Until the fourth century of the Christian era the Nativity and the Manifestation of Christ to the Gentiles were celebrated together on 6 January the Feast of the Epiphany. In that century, however, Pope Julius I (AD 337–52), after much careful inquiry, came to the conclusion that a very old tradition giving 25 December as the right date of the Birth was very probably true. This date already had a sacred significance for thousands of people throughout the Roman Empire because it was the *Dies Natalis Invicti Solis*, the Birthday of the Unconquered Sun, and also the chief festival of the Phrygian god, Attis, and of Mithras, the soldiers' god, whose cult was carried to Britain and many other countries by the Roman army. In the barbarian North, also, the long celebration of Yule, which lasted from November until January and included 25 December, was held at this season. The Church therefore, following its ancient practice of giving Christian meaning to pagan rituals wherever that was possible, and relying upon a tradition recorded by St Chrysostom and some others, eventually adopted 25 December for its own splendid festival, and so changed the age-old worship of the material sun, and the gods associated with it, to that of the true Light of the World.

Many of our modern Christmas customs are directly derived from pagan ceremonies belonging to ancient midwinter feasts. One of the oldest is probably the decoration of houses and churches with greenery. Evergreens, which are symbols of undying life, were commonly used to adorn the dwellings of our forefathers, and their sacred buildings, at the time of the winter solstice, and they have been so used ever since. It is true that, in the early years of Christianity, the Church forbade this practice because of its pagan origins, but the old custom was too strong to be easily uprooted, and gradually the first prohibitions lapsed and were forgotten. Holly and ivy were always favourite plants, as they are now, but formerly laurel and bays, inherited from the Roman Kalends of January, were also used, and so was rosemary, ilex, and sometimes cypress. ' Whatsoever the season of the yeare afforded to be greene ' said John Stow in his *Survey of London and Westminster* (1598), describing the decking of London's houses, churches, conduits, and street standards in his own and in former times.

Mistletoe was used in houses, but it was, and mostly still is, banned from the majority of churches. The Golden Bough of classical legend, sacred alike to the Druids and the Norsemen, the plant which slew Baldur the Beautiful, it was too strongly pagan to be allowed in any Christian church. Even now, it is rarely, if ever, seen there. In a few parishes, it may be permitted to hang in the porch, but if any is carried with the other greenery into the body of the church, it is usually removed immediately, as soon as its presence is realized. There have been exceptions to this rule, of which the best-known was the medieval ritual at York Minster. There, on Christmas Eve, a branch of mistletoe was ceremonially laid on the high altar, and left there all through the Twelve Days of Christmas. A universal pardon and liberty was proclaimed throughout the city for so long as it remained there.

The curious custom of kissing under the mistletoe seems to be altogether English in origin, and to appear in other countries only when Englishmen have taken it there. The old kissing bough, that lovely garland that used to hang from the ceiling of the living-room in so many houses before the coming of the Christmas tree, had a bunch of mistletoe attached to its base. It was a crown, or a globe, of greenery, adorned with lighted candles, red apples, rosettes and ribbons, with the mistletoe hanging below. Sometimes small presents were suspended from it, at the ends of long ribbon streamers. The Christmas tree superseded it in many homes in the middle of the last century, but it never faded away altogether, and can still sometimes be seen, especially in northern England, either by itself, or as an additional ornament in a room which already contains a tree.

The Christmas tree was a newcomer to England in the first half of the nineteenth century. It came originally from Germany, and went to America with the German settlers there before it reached the British Isles. How old it was in its country of origin before it set out on its travels to other lands is unknown; one legend associates it with St Boniface, the English missionary who preached to the heathen Germans in the eighth century; another says it was introduced into the homes of the people by Martin Luther. The first English tree of which we have any clear record was one set up at a children's party by a member of Queen Caroline's Court in 1821. Three more appeared at Panshanger in 1829, brought in for another children's party by Princess Lieven, who was staying there at the time. By 1840, William Howitt in his *The Rural Life of England* (2nd ed. 1840), could speak of the custom as quite well-known in Manchester, where it had been introduced by the German merchants who lived there, and had spread to their English neighbours. But what really established the foreign tree and made it one of our cherished Christmas customs was the setting-up by Prince Albert of a Christmas tree – the first of many – at Windsor Castle in 1841. This widely reported incident made the new custom known to everyone; and – slowly, because the English are a conservative race, reluctant to adopt new ways, but steadily – people began to follow the royal example, and to replace their English kissing boughs by continental trees. Within little more than twenty years, the latter were to be seen in countless homes, and hundreds were annually on sale at Covent

Garden Market. Now, a century later, it has overflowed from the houses into the streets and squares. Churches of every denomination have their lighted and decorated trees, proudly standing in the nave, or outside in the churchyard. St Paul's Cathedral has two, one in the portico, and the other just inside the west door. Both are the gifts of the Queen, and are grown on her estates. Since 1947, Oslo has made an annual gift to the people of London, in the form of an immense tree which stands, blazing with lights, in Trafalgar Square, close to Nelson's Monument.

Many churches now have a Christmas crib, though not so long ago this little model of the stable at Bethlehem, with its figures of the Holy Family and of animals, was rarely to be seen outside Roman Catholic churches and homes. Tradition says it was St Francis of Assisi who made the first crib, at Greccio in 1224. He did, in fact, make one in that year – or cause it to be made – but it was not the first of its kind. As far back as the eighth century, a permanent *presepio*, or crib, existed in the Church of Sta Maria Maggiore in Rome, and formed an essential part of the liturgical Office of the Shepherds at least as early as the eleventh century. But if St Francis was not the first to present the crib to the faithful, it was certainly he and his Franciscans who helped to make it widely known, and very popular in all Roman Catholic countries, especially Italy. Now, in England as elsewhere, the crib appears at Christmas not only in churches of various kinds, but also in many homes, and occasionally, rather surprisingly, in the windows of a few shops.

The giving of presents and the exchange of Christmas cards are almost equally essential parts of the Christmas festival today, though one has its roots in pre-Christian times, and the other is little more than a century old. Presents were given to kinsfolk and to the poor at the feast of the Saturnalia in pagan Rome, and so they were at the three-day Kalends of January, when the New Year was celebrated. The Christmas card began life in the late eighteenth century as the ' Christmas piece ', a decorated sheet of paper on which schoolchildren laboriously wrote polite greetings for the season in their best handwriting, to be presented to their parents at the end of the winter term. Sometimes, also, adults wrote complimentary verses – often of their own composition – for their friends on stationery still more elaborately ornamental; and it was from these two forms that the true Christmas card, as we know it today, developed.

This was an English invention, which later spread to the
United States of America and many other countries, but exactly
who was its inventor is still uncertain. More than one person
has claimed that honour, but it is now usually supposed that the
artist J. C. Horsley designed the first genuine pictorial card at
the instigation of Sir (then Mr) Henry Cole in 1843. Three years
later, when Summerley's *Home Treasury* office published Horsley's
design as a card priced at one shilling, only about a thousand
copies appear to have been sold; but if this number was small, it
was nevertheless the beginning of a steadily increasing stream
which, in our own day, has swelled to a torrent flowing all over
the world.

Father Christmas is the traditional gift-bringer in this country,
as, in his St Nicholas form, he is in many European lands, and as
Santa Claus in America. His has been a long and varied career.
Once he was Odin, riding on his eight-footed horse through
the world on dark and stormy nights in Yule, rewarding or
punishing his worshippers according to their deserts. When
Christianity swept away the old gods, his mantle fell upon
St Nicholas, who was Bishop of Myra during the fourth century.
Legend says of him that in his lifetime he was accustomed to
bestow anonymous gifts upon those most direly in need, and that
once he had saved three young girls from being sold into
prostitution by their poverty-stricken father. On three separate
nights, he came secretly to the house and dropped a bag of
gold through their window while they slept, each bag containing
enough gold to provide one of the girls with a marriage portion.
He is also said to have restored three schoolboys to life by a
miracle, after they had been murdered by an innkeeper. After his
death, he became the patron saint of children and also of captives
and sailors, all of whom he had helped in the most practical way
while he lived.

It is as a bishop that he now appears in Holland, Switzerland,
and some parts of Austria and Germany, wearing episcopal robes
and a mitre, and accompanied by a servant carrying a sack of
gifts. Quite often he is followed by a troop of masked demons
and other strange creatures. He never appears thus in England,
and though he is often called Santa Claus nowadays, not all who
call him so realize that he was either a bishop or a saint. The
original English Father Christmas was neither of these things,
and seems to have been more a personification of the joys of

Christmas than a gift-bringer. He is mentioned in a fifteenth-century carol which began, ' Hail, Father Christmas, hail to thee!', and he has been a familiar figure for centuries as one of the characters in some versions of the Mumming Play. Parliament abolished him in 1644, along with everything else connected with the Feast of Christmas, but he came back after the Restoration, and is still one of our living traditions. But he has changed somewhat in the 300 years that have elapsed since his return. In the nineteenth century, he acquired some of the attributes of the Teutonic Santa Klaus; and now expectant English children think of him as essentially the gift-bringer, coming by night from the Far North in his reindeer-drawn sleigh, and entering the houses he visits by way of the chimney.

A custom once very popular, and directly connected with St Nicholas as the patron saint of schoolboys, was that of the Boy Bishop. Seventy or eighty years ago, it might have been supposed quite dead in this country, but during the present century, a curious semi-revival seems to have taken place in some parts of England. In the Middle Ages, it was customary for the boy choristers of cathedrals, collegiate (and some parish) churches, and a few schools, to choose one of their number to act as their Bishop from St Nicholas's Day (6 December) to Holy Innocents' Day (28 December). During that time he had to perform, so far as he was able, most of the duties of an adult prelate. He wore episcopal robes, chose, and was attended by, other boys acting as his lesser clergy, sang Vespers, and took a chief part in all the church services, except those which only an ordained priest could celebrate. Throughout his term of office, he was treated by everyone, layman and cleric alike, with great respect, received many generous gifts, and was lavishly entertained. On his last day as bishop, he was required to preach a sermon, and to ride out in procession to bless the people.

This custom was suppressed by Henry VIII in 1541, and although Mary I revived it in 1554, her successor, Elizabeth, abolished it once more. In Europe, it did not long survive the Reformation in Protestant countries, and, though in Roman Catholic lands it declined more slowly, it had vanished almost everywhere by the end of the eighteenth century. Then, in 1899, the Rev. H. K. Hudson, at that time Vicar of Berden, in Essex, started a modern form of Boy Bishop ceremony in his parish, and maintained it until he left Berden in 1937. Since then, a modified version of the old ritual has appeared in several parishes, often, rather oddly, in conjunction with a May Queen. The boy chosen to act as bishop is expected to act as leader of the children in all church matters, and to undertake certain defined duties during his term of office, though he is no longer called upon to officiate in the services, or to preach a sermon. It may be noticed that in some of the churches which have, or did have until recently, under some former vicar, a Boy Bishop in the Christmas season, the custom is not so much a ' revival ' as a ' borrowing ', since in many instances, no such practice seems to have been observed in the parish concerned in pre-Reformation times.

As long as domestic fires customarily burned on great, open hearths, the Yule Log was one of the main features of the Christmas festivities in England, as in many other European countries. Our small modern grates do not, of course, permit the observance of this ancient custom, and it is only very rarely seen now. The traditional log was usually of oak or ash, and as large as the widest fireplace in the house would allow. It was brought in on Christmas Eve with ceremony and rejoicing, and lit with a fragment of its predecessor of the year before. It had to burn steadily for a fixed time, usually the whole of the Twelve Days of Christmas, and if, by some disastrous chance, it went out during that period, the omen for the coming year was very bad. At the end of the time it was quenched, and a portion carefully put by to use in kindling next year's log, so that there might be continuity of blessing in that house. It was never, under any circumstances, allowed to burn away completely.

In Devon and Somerset, the Ashen Faggot was a well-known substitute for the Yule Log. This was – or indeed, is, for it is still made in some places – a large faggot of green ash sticks, very thick in the middle, and tightly bound with bands of ash or hazel. In private houses it was (and probably still is) usual for young people to choose a band and name it for themselves; if it was the first to break in the heat of the fire, then its ' owner ' would be the first of the company to marry. At inns, the breaking of the first band was a signal for a round of free drinks. Ashen Faggots are still burnt in some old inns, or farmhouses, which have the necessary deep and wide hearths, and elsewhere the memory of the custom is often preserved by the use of miniature faggots on small, modern grates.

Christmas food has always been largely a matter of tradition, but its nature has changed a great deal with the passage of time. The turkey which is now the most usual dish on Christmas Day did not appear in this country until about 1542, and did not really become popular until much later. Its predecessors were goose, or pork, or beef, or sometimes a huge Christmas pie made up of a variety of birds. In the greater houses, venison, swans, or bustards were eaten, or peacocks in their feathers, with their tails spread and their beaks gilded. Chief over all was the boar's head, that splendid dish of pagan ancestry, which was always brought to the table with immense ceremony, garlanded, often heralded by the sound of trumpets, and borne in upon the finest platter of gold or silver that the household could provide.

At the Queen's College, Oxford, boar's head has been served thus at Christmas time since as far back as the late fourteenth century. The head is decorated with rosemary, bay, and holly, and has an orange thrust between its teeth. Four men carry it in upon a silver basin; the chief singer, who sings the verses of ' The Boar's Head Carol ', goes before them, and behind them come the choristers, who sing the refrain. This carol was already old when Wynkyn de Worde printed it in 1521. On its way up through the Hall, the procession halts three times to allow the chief singer to sing one of the verses, and then moves forward again while the refrain is sung. When the High Table is finally reached, the head is set before the Provost, who removes the orange from its mouth, and presents it to the chief singer. The green sprigs (some gilded), with which the head is adorned, are then taken from it and distributed among the principal guests.

An odd legend supposedly accounts for the annual perform-ance of this ceremony. Long ago, it is said, a scholar of the Queen's College, whose name was Copcot, was walking alone and unarmed in Shotover Forest, and was suddenly confronted by a wild boar. In this dangerous situation he, with great presence of mind, thrust a copy of Aristotle, which he had with him, down the boar's throat, crying as he did so, ' Swallow that if you can!' The astonished boar replied ' *Graecum est* ', and forthwith died. In commemoration of this incident, the Boar's Head cere-mony is supposed to take place yearly. But in fact, it is more probably a survival from the days when the Queen's College students, being mostly Westmorland and Cumberland men, had to eat their Christmas feast in Oxford because the vacation was then too short to allow them to make the long, slow journey to their homes and back again.

The ancestor of our modern Christmas pudding was plum porridge. This was a mixture of meat broth, raisins, spices, fruit juice, and wine, thickened by brown breadcrumbs, and served in a semi-liquid state at the beginning of the meal. By about 1670, it had stiffened into the pudding we know, and doubtless had already become the repository of secret wishes which it still is today. Wherever puddings are made at home, every member of the family is normally expected to take a hand in the stirring, for luck, and it is then that the wish should be made; but like most magical wishes, its nature must not be revealed to anyone, or it will not be granted. By right, a few small charms ought to be included in the mixture – a silver coin promising wealth to the person who finds it in his portion on Christmas Day, a ring denoting speedy marriage, a thimble prophesying a single life, or any other small object from which the future can be read. The pudding itself must be crowned with a sprig of scarlet-berried holly before it is brought to the table and, if possible, have flaming brandy on it.

Mince pies are older than plum pudding, and were already well known by the end of the sixteenth century. They were much more varied in content then and less sweet than they are now, consisting of chopped or minced chicken, neats' tongues or mutton, eggs, spices and raisins, all contained in little pastry cases known as ' coffins '. Tradition has it that if anyone eats one of these pies on each of the Twelve Days of Christmas, he or she will have twelve happy months in the coming year. As for drinks, there does not appear to be any special ceremonial Christmas drink now, unless it is hot punch, but once there was Lambs' Wool. This was a truly splendid beverage, made of hot ale, sugar, spices, eggs, roasted apples, and thick cream. Few people would serve so lordly a dish at their table now, but some of the great bowls once used for the purpose still survive, such as the immense silver-gilt bowl at Jesus College, Oxford, which holds ten gallons at a time, and has a ladle that takes half a pint.

Carols, with their simple and lovely words and their dancing tunes, mean only Christmas for most of us now, though there are also carols for Easter, and Whitsun, and for May Day. They are not, and never have been, hymns in the ordinary sense of that word; rather, they are the popular songs of the Christian religion which came into being after the religious revival of the thirteenth century, and flourished most strongly in the three centuries that followed. There were, of course, carols before this, songs with lilting tunes, as befitted the original meaning of the name, which was to dance and sing in a ring. Many of the earlier ones were purely secular and festive, concerned with love and courtship, or the return of summer, as the May carol is, or some other cheerful theme. They were, by nature, happy songs, and so usually were the religious carols that followed them into popularity in the late fourteenth and early fifteenth centuries.

Puritanism swept away the English carols during the Commonwealth and, rather strangely, they did not come back into general favour for about 200 years afterwards. They never died out altogether, but they led a kind of underground life, never heard in churches or in well-to-do houses, but only amongst simple and unlettered folk. In his *Every Day Book* (1826) William Hone calls them ' ditties which now exclusively enliven the industrious servant-maid and the humble labourer. . . .' He might also have mentioned the Waits, who often included carols in the music they played round the towns on their oboes, serpents, clarinets, and fiddles. These Waits were originally watchmen, who patrolled the streets at night and at intervals called out the time; but later, the name was applied to the town band, musicians who played for civic ceremonies and processions, and could also be engaged by ordinary people to play for weddings and other private occasions. Towards the end of the eighteenth century, many towns abolished their official Waits for economic reasons, but the name then passed to any group of musicians who went about at Christmas time and played outside the different houses of the township.

When Hone wrote, most people believed that before long carols would have disappeared completely, but in fact, the first step towards their rehabilitation had already been taken. In 1822 Davis Gilbert published the first modern collection of carols, and in 1833 William Sandys produced another. Both these men thought it necessary to collect and record what they could before carol singing became extinct. In 1852, two clergymen, J. E. Neale and T. Helmore, came by a rare Swedish book named *Piae Cantiones* which contained many lovely sixteenth-century carols. Some of these they published in *Carols for Christmas-tide*. Others followed in the work of collecting, including, in the last decade of the century Cecil Sharp; and slowly, but steadily, after two centuries of eclipse, the English Christmas carol came into its own again.

Now, nearly all churches have their carol service. In many towns, the people gather round the communal Christmas tree, or in the town hall, to sing under the leadership of the local clergy, or of the mayor. Every year, on Christmas Eve, the lovely ceremony of the Nine Lessons is broadcast from King's College Chapel in Cambridge. Nine sets of carols are sung there, alternating with passages from the Gospel story, all of it sung and spoken in a chapel lit only by candlelight. Outside ordinary front doors, small groups appear, perhaps the church choir come out into the open, or a glee club, or the members of some other local organization, singing for charity. And, of course, there are the children, who come round, like the Waits before them, collecting money for themselves. They do not sing very well as a rule, and are usually too hurried to sing the whole carol through before ringing the bell, but all the same, they are still, like their medieval forerunners, the bearers of the Good News, and it would be a pity if their thin young voices were heard no more in the nights before Christmas.

Sometimes hand-bell ringers accompany the carol-singers, or go round alone making their Christmas music. At one time, almost every parish had its team of hand-bell ringers, and many still do, though the old ringing custom is now less usual than it once was. The pealing of church bells, that most English of sounds, is an important part of the English Christmas season, from St Thomas's Day, when their clamour is said to ' ring in Christmas ', through Christmas Eve and Day, and on to the New Year. A curious bell custom is kept up at Dewsbury, in Yorkshire, where, on Christmas Eve, the tenor bell in the parish church is tolled once for every year since Christ was born in Bethlehem. The ringing is timed to end exactly at midnight, and so usher in Christmas Day. This custom is known as Ringing the Devil's Knell, or the Old Lad's Passing Bell, because, as it is locally explained, ' the Devil died when Christ was born ', or, according to another form of the tradition, the sound of the bell keeps Satan away from Dewsbury folk during the coming year. Legend says that the bell-ringing began in the late thirteenth or early fourteenth century, when Sir Thomas de Soothill established the custom in expiation of a murder he had committed. Little is known about Sir Thomas, and less about the murder; but the bell he gave to the parish church is still faithfully rung, and every year one more stroke is added to the ever-growing record of the years.

St Stephen's Day is 26 December, the feast of St Stephen, the first Christian martyr. But in England this anniversary is far better known as Boxing Day, a name derived either from the alms boxes in churches, which were opened, and their contents distributed to the poor on that day; or from the earthenware boxes that apprentices used to carry round with them when they were collecing money gifts from their master's customers. Until very recently it was usual for the postman, the dustman, and a few other servants of the public to call at all the houses they had served during the year, and to receive small gifts from the householders on Boxing Day. Perhaps because so many people now go away for Christmas, or because of the general rise in the level of wages, this custom is steadily declining, and it is probable that before very long, the old friendly habit will have disappeared for good.

Formerly, indeed, it was very widespread. Not only postmen and dustmen, but also lamplighters, turncocks, road-sweepers, errand boys and many more came round asking for their Christmas boxes. Apprentices, shop assistants, and errand boys did very well, for they first received a gift from their own master, and then made the round of his customers, to collect further gifts from them. In country parishes, the sexton and the bell-ringers sometimes came too. Household servants, of course, usually had their presents with the family, on Christmas Day or Eve; if not, they expected them on Boxing Day. A pleasant custom, now unhappily quite forgotten, was the remitting by innkeepers of part of the charges for all meals served on 26 December.

In the Isle of Man, a part of the old Wren Hunt ritual still survives on St Stephen's Day, though in a very fragmentary form. Bands of boys, usually three or four in number, go about the town or village, singing a version of the ' Wren Song ', and collecting money from the people whose houses they visit. Their leader carries a green garland on a pole, and the others usually have staves decorated with leaves and ribbons. But the Wren which was once carried in the garland is missing, and nothing represents it any longer; and only the words of the ' Wren Song ' (rather gabbled and not very clear, as a rule) indicate what this visit of the boys is all about.

In fact, it is a last fading trace of the famous Wren Hunt

which once flourished in many parts of England, especially in the south and west, Wales, Ireland, the Isle of Man, and France. The wren, the King of the Birds, was one of those sacred birds, like the robin and the swallow, who must never be harmed, nor their nests damaged or destroyed. ' Kill a robin or a wren, Never prosper, boy or man ', runs a Devonshire proverb, and on the other side of England, in Essex, they say :

> The robin and the redbreast,
> The robin and the wren,
> If ye tak' out of the nest,
> Ye'll never thrive again.

Yet once a year this sacred and honoured bird was fiercely hunted and killed, and its corpse paraded about the district on the top of a pole, or in the centre of a cross-hooped garland. In a few places, notably in Pembrokeshire, the wren was not killed, but was carried round in a cage, or a ' wren-house ', and afterwards released. In most cases, however, it died, and the man or boy who was the first to kill one of these little creatures was honoured, in some areas as king for the day, in others as a temporary leader, and one likely to be lucky throughout the year.

' On St Stephen's Day ', wrote John Kelly in his *English and Manx Dictionary*, compiled about 1790, ' the inhabitants of this district assemble to hunt the little wren, which, when caught and killed, they fasten to the top of a long pole and carry about in procession, with drums beating and colours flying, and distribute for money the feathers of the bird, which are esteemed by the purchasers to be a charm against all evils for the ensuing year.' Sailors especially prized them, believing they were a protection against shipwreck, and sometimes the carcase of the dead bird was carried on to one of the boats of the fishing fleet, as a luck bringer. It is, however, a long time now since any living Manx Wren was hunted to its death on St Stephen's day, and all that now remains of the old ritual there is the empty garland, and the boys going about hopefully, singing,

> The Wren, the Wren, the King of all birds,
> On St Stephen's Day was caught in the furze,
> Although he is little, his family is great,
> I pray you, good dame, do give us a treat.

# 2 The Opening Year

THE NEW YEAR COMES IN very merrily in most parts of England, with the pealing of bells and the blowing of ships' sirens and train whistles, and the gallant attempts of English people to sing *Auld Lang Syne*, which they know to be the traditional song for the festival, but of which the majority know only some of the words, and those not very well. In London, great crowds assemble outside St Paul's Cathedral to see the Old Year out and welcome in the New. Private parties are held everywhere, at home or in hotels, lively toasts are drunk, and good wishes exchanged. Some celebrate the occasion more quietly, and see the New Year in at a Watch Night service in some Anglican or Nonconformist church. This is now quite a widespread custom, though it dates only from the eighteenth century, and was started by the Methodist Society, from which it spread to other communions. In a few parishes, the service is followed by the singing of hymns on the top of the church tower. All this, and several other still-existing customs, bear witness to the fact that, for most of us,

New Year's Day is a very important date, the beginning of a fresh year, a clean white page on which splendid and happy things may yet be written. Better times are coming, we hope, in both senses of that phrase; and so we make yet another set of good resolutions, in spite of past experience, and enjoy ourselves as much as we can at the year's start, in the half-acknowledged, but all the same, general belief that as the beginning is, so will all the rest be.

In the north of England, as in Scotland and some European countries, the custom of First-footing still flourishes. The First Foot is the first visitor to any house in the morning hours of 1 January. He is the luck-bringer, and no one must be admitted before he comes; when he arrives, he must be brought in through the front door, and welcomed with plentiful supplies of food and drink, especially the latter. He brings with him symbolic gifts which vary a little in different places, but are most usually a piece of bread and a lump of coal, salt, and a little money, all of which together ensure that his hosts will have food and warmth and prosperity all through the year. If he is a vigorous and upstanding young man, and especially if he is good looking, the omen is doubly good, but in any case, he must be a man with certain definite and clearly recognizable qualities.

He must be dark-haired, at least in most districts. In some parts of north-eastern England he must, on the contrary be fair, but only very occasionally is red hair considered lucky. He must not be cross-eyed, or flat-footed, or have eyebrows meeting across his nose. Often he is a friend of the family visited, who has arranged to come as soon as possible after midnight, or sometimes a man with the right qualifications will go round in turn to every house in a particular area. If not such a visitor is available, the master of the house may have to be his own First Foot (or some other male in-dweller may have to act for him), going outside just before midnight, and being ceremonially re-admitted, with the magical gifts in his hand, as soon as the clock has struck. The visit of a woman, whether as official First Foot, or simply because she happens to call before any man has come to let the New Year in, is very unlucky almost everywhere in England, though in parts of Wales and in the Isle of Man it is sometimes permissible.

At Allendale, in Northumberland, the New Year is welcomed by a fire ceremony, followed by First-footing. A great bonfire is built in the main square and left, for the time being, unlit. Near it a silver band plays, while the Guisers, in their gay costumes, go round the village and call at all the public houses. Then, a little before midnight, they line up to form a procession, each man carrying a blazing tar barrel on his head. Thus crowned with flames and billowing smoke, and preceded by the band, they march to the bonfire, having circuited it, throw their burning barrels on it, and so set it alight. The spectators cheer and sing, and everyone rejoices, and then, as soon as the bonfire has burnt down a little, the Guisers go off First-footing all round the parish.

Another New Year custom, gone now, but still known in Herefordshire at the beginning of this century, was Burning the Bush. Every farm formerly had its Bush, or hawthorn globe which, together with a bunch of mistletoe, hung in the farmhouse kitchen all through the year, from one New Year's Day to the next. At about five o'clock in the morning on 1 January, it was taken down, carried out to the first-sown wheatfield, and there burnt on a large straw fire. On some farms, once the globe had been set alight, it was carried, flaming, by a fast-running man over the first twelve ridges of the field. In others, burning straw from the fire itself was used instead. It was considered very unlucky if the flames went out before the twelfth ridge was reached. Then, all the men concerned in the affair made a ring round the fire and cried ' Auld-Ci-der ', very slowly, on a single deep note, repeating each syllable three times, and bowing low as each one was uttered. Afterwards there was cheering, and the drinking of the farmer's health, and feasting upon cider and plum cake, either then and there on the field, or later, inside the farmhouse. Meanwhile, a new Bush, or globe, was being made at home and hung up in place of the old. All this was supposed to bring good luck to the crops, and at one time, it was firmly believed that, without these rituals, the corn would not grow. A similar, but less elaborate ceremony was known in Worcestershire, where a crown of blackthorn was used instead of the hawthorn bush, and was said to represent the Crown of Thorns.

A curious little ceremony is observed on 1 January at the Queen's College, Oxford. The Bursar presents each member of the College then present with a needle threaded with coloured silk, saying as he does so, ' Take this and be thrifty '. This needle and thread – in French *aiguille et fil* – is a punning reference to Robert de Eglesfield, who founded the College in 1341, and directed that he should be remembered in this strange manner.

He intended that every member of the College, senior and junior, should share his small gift and his advice, but as the majority of the students are normally away from Oxford on 1 January, it is mainly the Fellows and their guests who receive both.

At All Souls' College, Oxford, they Hunt the Mallard once in every century, on 14 January. The Mallard in question is the tutelary bird of All Souls which, according to legend, was flushed from a drain while the foundations of the College were being laid in 1437, and flew away. Hence, on Mallard Night, it is vigorously sought for in every corner of the building, up and down stairs and out over the roof. The hunters are all the Fellows, led by an elected Lord Mallard and six attendants of his own choosing. The Hunt takes place at midnight and is lit by torches; and as they go, the whole company sing the Mallard Song, of which the chorus runs:

> O, by the blood of King Edward,
> O, by the blood of King Edward,
> It was a swapping, swapping Mallard!

It would be interesting to know which King Edward is intended, but nobody seems to do so, though various theories have been put forward. Nor is it known for certain how long this ceremony has been observed. Tradition says it is nearly as old as the College itself, but the first actual mention of it occurs in a letter from Archbishop Abbot, written in 1632, and bitterly complaining of a ' great outrage ' committed by the College, involving riotous behaviour ' under pretence of a foolish mallard '. Originally, it was an annual event associated with the Feast, or Gaudy, on 14 January. It seems to have lapsed at some time in the eighteenth century, for Thomas Hearne, writing in his *Diary* in 1722, says it had not been held for some years then, though the Mallard Song was still sung at the Gaudy, but by 1801 it was evidently in full swing again, even if not held annually, as of old. Bishop Heber, then at Brasenose, just opposite All Souls, watched from his garret window ' the Lord Mallard and about forty fellows in a kind of procession on the library roof, with immense lighted torches, which had a singular effect '. He heard them singing as they went on, and his widow's *Life of Heber* reports he remarked that ' all who had the gift of hearing within half a mile must have been awakened by the manner in which they thundered their chorus, " O, by the blood of King Edward ".' It has since become an established tradition that the Mallard Hunt takes place once in every century, at the beginning and on 14 January. It was last held in 1901, and will be due again in 2001.

Twelfth Night and Twelfth Day – 5 and 6 January – are popularly so called because they mark the end of the Twelve Days of Christmas. In their own right, they are the Vigil and Feast of the Epiphany, that ancient festival which is older than Christmas, and was not separated from it until about the middle of the fourth century. The Twelve Days which link these two great feasts were for many centuries a time, not only of religious devotion, but also of holiday and high revelry, when only the minimum of necessary work was done, and many customary regulations were relaxed. We are not now so robust, or so generous as our forefathers, and 12 days of continuous rejoicing is perhaps more than we can stand, or are willing to allow to others. At all events, over the last two centuries, the 12-day period has steadily shrunk, and now only two days – Christmas Day and its ' morrow ', Boxing Day – remain as official holidays. However, from 1974 onwards, New Year's Day is to become once more an English holiday, as it was long ago. (In Scotland, of course, it has been, ever since the Reformation, a very great festival occasion, far more important for most people than Christmas.)

Not so long ago, bonfires were lit on Twelfth Night in many parts of the West Midlands, often 12 in number, with one made larger than the rest, to represent Our Lord and His Apostles. Sometimes there were 13, and then the 13th, standing for Judas Iscariot, was stamped out soon after it was lit. In Herefordshire and south-west Worcestershire, on the same night, the wassail bowl was carried out to the cattle byre, together with a large plum cake with a hole in its centre. After the oxen had been toasted in cider, the cake was hung on the horns of the best ox, and he was encouraged to toss his head and throw it off. If it fell forward, the omen for the farm was good, and the bailiff claimed the cake for himself; if it fell backwards, the mistress had it, and the omen was less fortunate. After these, and similar Twelfth Night customs elsewhere, a supper was usually held in the farmhouse for all the men on the farm.

No one lights these bonfires now, nor wassails their cattle, but there is one time-honoured Twelfth Night custom which still lingers in the West Country. In a few parishes of Devon and Somerset, the apple trees are wassailed, as of old, to make them bear abundantly. The owner of the trees and his men go down to the orchard after dusk, carrying shot-guns and a large pail of cider. One particular tree, a good one, is usually chosen to represent them all; cider is poured round its roots, and pieces of toast soaked in cider are laid in the fork. The shot-guns are fired through the branches, and a traditional wassailing song is sung. This song has several variants, but all make the object of the ceremony quite clear. ' Here's to thee, auld apple tree ', says one version,

> Whence thou may'st bud and whence thou may'st blow,
> And whence thou may'st bear apples enow,
> Hats full, caps full,
> Bushel, bushel sacks full,
> And my pockets full too!

At one time, the apple-wassailing custom existed in many parts of southern England, and in the West Midlands also. It sometimes took place at Christmas, or on New Year's Eve, but Twelfth Night was the favourite date for it. Now it has vanished from all but a few places, and where it survives, it has often become more of a frolic than anything else by now. Nevertheless, it is generally considered to be very unlucky to omit it, which is a sure sign of something that was once a serious rite. At Carhampton and at Roadwater, both in Somerset, the wassailing takes place on Old Twelfth Night, which is 17 January.

The centre-piece of the Twelfth-tide feast in its heyday was a cake of great magnificence which contained a bean and a pea. The bean was very important because the man who got it in his slice became King of the Bean, sometimes known as the Epiphany King, and lord of the revels for as long as the feast lasted. The girl who found the pea in her share became the Queen; but sometimes the pea was omitted altogether, and the Queen was chosen either by the King himself, or by some man who found the pea in his own slice, and so acquired the right of selecting the Queen.

The Bean ceremony died away slowly in England during the eighteenth century, but the cake itself remained popular for at least another half century. A little before the anniversary came round, all the pastry-cooks' windows in London and the bigger towns began to fill with cakes, large and small – rich, dark cakes, full of fruit, heavily iced, and lavishly decorated with stars and dragons, flowers, crowns, and little figures of the Three Kings, whose season Twelfth-tide is. They were a splendid sight to see in the shop window, or on the dining-table, and they were much admired; but by about the middle of the nineteenth century they were already giving way before the later, and less exotic Christmas cake, and now they are only very rarely seen.

One well-known survivor of a nearly forgotten tradition there is the famous Baddeley Cake which commemorates Robert Baddeley of Drury Lane. He was a chef who subsequently became an actor, a member of the Drury Lane company, and did very well in his new profession. When he died in 1794, he left £100 for the provision of wine and a Twelfth Cake to be shared on Twelfth Night every year by the company then acting at Drury Lane Theatre. On 6 January, therefore, after the stage performance has ended, the great cake is ceremonially brought to the Green Room by the theatre attendants in their eighteenth-century liveries, and cut in the presence of the assembled actors. Each receives his or her portion (though there is no bean or pea in it to look out for), and all drink the health of the man whose ambition it had been to become one of their company.

The Hood Game, which is played at Haxey, in the Isle of Axeholme, every year on 6 January, is an old and very interesting game, almost certainly much older than it is locally supposed to be. Legend asserts that it was first played there in the thirteenth century, after Lady Mowbray had lost her scarlet hood in a gale, whilst riding from Haxey to Westwoodside. Twelve labourers, working nearby, rushed after it, and eventually managed to catch it, though not without great difficulty, for the boisterous wind kept snatching it from their outstretched hands. In gratitude for the restoration of her hood, and also, it is said, for the amusement the men's antics in retrieving it had afforded her, Lady Mowbray gave 13 half-acres of land to the parish, to provide for a hood to be played for annually on the same day for ever, and for a feast to follow the game. This story is supposed to account for the existence of the game, and for the red colour associated with the dress of the players; but from the nature of the contest itself and from the ceremonies attached to it, it seems more likely that originally it was part of an ancient seasonal ritual connected with the end of the midwinter festival, and the fertilization of the newly ploughed fields. If the tale of Lady Mowbray is anything more than one of those aetiological legends which do often spring up to account for persistent customs of which the true meaning has been forgotten, it may have its roots in a gift of land made in the thirteenth century to endow a game already well established then. Of the 13 half-acres said to have been given, only one can now be traced. Here the lady is supposed to have lost her hood, and here now, the first Hood of the game is always thrown up. The whereabouts of the other 12 is unknown, and all the deeds relating to them have disappeared.

The official players are the 12 Boggons, of whom the chief is the King Boggon, or Lord of the Hood. Tradition requires them all to wear red-flannel coats and red flowers in their hats, and some still do. Others compromise with a red shirt or pullover, but all have something red about them, even if it is only a scarlet armband. The King Boggon carries a wand of 13 willows bound with 13 withy-bands as a badge of office. The Fool, who leads the preliminary procession, has his trousers patched with pieces of red cloth, a red shirt, or coat, and flowers in his hat. His face is smeared with soot and red ochre, and he carries a whip and a cock filled with bran at the end of the thong. The Hood round which the game centres bears no resemblance to any sort of headgear, but is a 2ft piece of thick rope encased in leather. This is the Leather, or Sway, Hood, which the Lord of the Hood carries; there are also a number of lesser Hoods made of tightly rolled canvas tied round with ribbons.

On Hood Day, the proceedings begin in the early afternoon with a procession of Boggons led by the Fool. They go to the small green by the church, and there the Fool is hoisted on to a stone that was once the base of the churchyard cross. He makes a speech welcoming those present and inviting them to join in the game, tells his audience, very mysteriously, that two bullocks and a half have been killed, but the other half is still running about the field, and finally reminds them of the rules of the game,

> Hoose agen hoose,
> Toon agen toon,
> If tho' meet a man, knock 'im doon,
> But don't 'ut 'im!

Meanwhile, a fire of damp straw is lit behind the Fool, and he is soon enveloped in clouds of smoke. This is the ceremony known as Smoking the Fool, which suggests a form of ritual fumigation. When it is over, he jumps down from the stone, and leads the Boggons and the crowd up to the high ground where the Hood Game begins.

First, the canvas Hoods are thrown up, one at a time. The Boggons and the crowd up to the high ground where the Hood men from various parts of the wide parish, standing inside the circle. The Lord of the Hood throws up the first Hood, and all the players (other than the Boggons) scramble for it, each man trying to get it outside the ring and away to his own part of the parish. If he succeeds, he keeps the Hood, but success is not easy. Not only must he elude all the other contestants who try to take it from him, but he must also get it past the waiting Boggons, who are there precisely to prevent the Hood from being carried away. If one of them so much as touches it during the struggle, it is at once out of the game, and has to be thrown up again.

The real business of the day starts at about four o'clock, when the Sway begins. The Leather, or Sway Hood is thrown up by the Lord, or by some distinguished visitor, the Boggon ring breaks up, and everyone in the crowd rushes forward in a wild attempt to seize the Hood and take it down the hill to one of the three inns in the parish. A solid mass of grimly earnest men, like a giant rugby scrum, pushes and drags and pulls the Leather Hood – they are not allowed by the rules to kick or throw it – edging it inch by inch downwards, first one way and then the other, each man struggling with all his strength to get it to his own village inn. Everything in the path of the slowly moving Sway goes down before it, including fences and hedges, and even stone walls. Eventually one or other of the inns is reached, though it may take a couple of hours or more to achieve this, and the Hood is given into the charge of the landlord, who will keep it until next Haxey Hood Day comes round.

This is the game which Lady Mowbray is locally supposed to have started one windy day in the thirteenth century. In fact, all the internal evidence points to its being rooted in pre-Christian antiquity. The red in the Boggon's dress, the importance of the Fool and the Smoking ceremony in which he is involved, the reference to the killing of the bullocks in the opening speech, and the fierce character of the struggle for the Leather Hood, all suggest that here we have a memory of an ancient contest between rival groups for the head, or half, of a sacrificial bull that had been slaughtered to bring fertility to the fields.

The Monday after Twelfth Day is Plough Monday, once a day of rural festivity, especially in the northern counties and the Midlands. Theoretically, work started again then on the farm, after the end of the Twelve Days of Christmas, and the spring ploughing began, but in fact, very little work was done. The ploughmen were out, not in the fields, but in the streets, drawing or following a decorated plough from house to house and collecting alms. This plough was called the Fool Plough, or sometimes the White Plough; the men themselves were known as Plough Stots or Plough Bullocks, Plough Jags, or Plough Witches, varying with the district in which they lived. They were accompanied on their rounds by a Fool, a man in woman's dress called the Bessy, or Besom-Bet, and often by the local Sword-dancers. At this season also, a version of the ancient Plough Monday Play used to be acted in some places. The procession went round the village with fiddles playing and horns blowing, stopping every now and then to dance their ritual sword figures, and demanding money from householders and passers-by alike. If they were refused alms at any house, the ground or the garden in front of that house was promptly ploughed up, which in a possibly wet and muddy January was not amusing. Such at least was the tradition wherever the Plough Monday festival was observed, but there does not seem to be any record of the outraged householder retaliating in any way.

In the Middle Ages, the various ploughmen's guilds often maintained a Plough Light in the church, and some of the money gained on Plough Monday went to support it. The Reformation destroyed the Light and the guilds, but the traditional festivities continued until well into the nineteenth century. They have gone now but, within our century, the old blessing by the Church of the plough and its work has been revived. On Plough Sunday, the eve of the old festival, a plough is brought to the church in many parishes, and placed in the chancel, where it is blessed in the presence of the local farmers, ploughmen, farm workers, and all the congregation.

Many people think that the Christmas decorations ought always to be taken down at Twelfth-tide, and some believe that it is

C

very unlucky not to do this. In fact, if luck is really in question, it is nothing of the sort, for if the Twelve Days of Christmas are ended, Christmas itself is not. The ecclesiastical Christmas season runs on till Candlemas Eve (1 February), and once it was not unusual to leave house decorations up till then. It was of Candlemas Eve that Herrick sang in his ' Hesperides ' :

> Down with the Rosemary and Bayes,
> Down with the Mistletoe;
> Instead of Holly, now upraise
> The greener Box for show.

> The Holly hitherto did sway;
> Let Box now domineere,
> Until the dancing Easter Day,
> Or Easter's Eve appeare.

The notion that it brings ill-luck to leave the Christmas greenery hanging after 6 January is comparatively modern, and probably owes as much to dislike of dusty and shrivelled evergreens as to anything else.

On 2 February, the double feast of the Presentation of Christ in the Temple and the Purification of Our Lady is celebrated. It is popularly known as Candlemas Day because candles are blessed in the churches then, distributed to the congregations, and carried in procession. This custom has existed in the Christian Church since as far back as the fifth century, and seems to have been at least partly derived from the pagan Feast of Lights which used to be observed on 1 February. At Blidworth, in Nottinghamshire, an old and beautiful custom commemorating the Presentation of Our Lord was revived in 1923 after a long post-Reformation lapse, and has been observed ever since. This is the Cradle-Rocking ceremony, which is said to have been known there in the thirteenth century, and now takes place on the Sunday nearest Candlemas Day. The parents of the boy baby most recently baptized in the parish present the child to the vicar, who lays him in an old wooden cradle, decorated with leaves and flowers, which has been placed in the chancel, near the altar. During the service, he blesses him, and gently rocks him in the cradle for a few moments. Then, at the end of the service, the baby is given back to his parents, while the choir sing the *Nunc Dimittis*.

The day after Candlemas is the Feast of St Blaise, who is the patron saint of wool-combers, and of all who suffer from diseases of the throat. He was a physician who became Bishop of Sebaste in Armenia, and was martyred there in or about AD 316. Legend says that he loved animals, both wild and tame, and had great power over them. Once, during a time of persecution, when he was forced to fly to the mountains and take refuge in a cavern, wild beasts used to come to his cave, seeking his blessing, and to be cured of their wounds or sicknesses. He became the patron saint of wool-combers because, before his execution by beheading, he suffered the horrible pains of having his flesh torn by small sharp implements, very like the combs used in one of the processes of cloth-making. Until the beginning of the nineteenth century, his day was kept as a general holiday in nearly all the wool towns of England and Scotland. Magnificent pageants and processions were held on these days, with St Blaise riding on horseback and dressed as a bishop, together with other wool heroes, like Jason and his Argonauts, Castor and Pollux, Jack of Newbury, and many more. Everyone even remotely connected with the wool trade played his or her part in the parades, from shepherds and sheep-shearers up to master combers and rich wool-staplers. At Bradford in Yorkshire, the Blaise celebration took place only once in seven years, and here the last (and very splendid) procession was held in 1825. This was almost the last regular celebration to be held in England; one which occurred in Norwich in 1836 was a revival, organized on the occasion of the foundation of a new yarn factory.

When St Blaise was being led away to the imprisonment that ended with his death, he saw a child choking on a fish bone that had become immovably fixed in his throat. The saint stopped and touched the boy's throat, and instantly the bone was dislodged, thus saving the child's life. It is this legend which accounts for St Blaise's reputation as a healer of throat troubles of all sorts. The beautiful ceremony of Blessing the Throat takes place on his day in many continental and some English Roman Catholic churches, including St Etheldreda's Church in Ely Place, London. Two long, blessed candles, tied together with ribbons in the form of a St Andrew's Cross, are used. The ribbon cross is laid under the chin of the patient, as he or she kneels before the altar, and the throat is gently touched with the ends of the lighted candles. As he does this, the officiating priest says, ' May the Lord deliver you from the evil of the throat, and from every other evil.' Many come every year to this and other churches where the service is held, to be cured of their ills on St Blaise's Day.

Of another famous February saint, St Valentine, little is known except that he has been regarded from time immemorial as the friend and patron of lovers, and on his feast day, 14 February, sweethearts were formerly chosen, and love tokens exchanged. There were, in fact, two saints of the same name, both of whom were martyred in the third century (though in different years) on 14 February, the Eve of the Roman Lupercalia. It is not certain which of these two is the lover's saint, nor why either should be supposed to be so. It is, however, a very old custom to choose sweethearts on their anniversary, the day on which, according to an ancient country tradition, all the birds also choose their mates.

One method of choice was by drawing lots. Names inscribed upon wooden billets or pieces of paper were placed in a vessel of some sort, and then drawn in turn by those present until every person had become someone's Valentine. Another notion, common in some districts, was that the first man seen by a woman on the festival morning was automatically her Valentine, whether she liked him or not. Great care, therefore had to be taken to avoid seeing the wrong man. Pepys records in his *Diary* for 1662 that Mrs Pepys was forced to go about her house with her eyes covered on 14 February, because there were painters working in it, and she was afraid of seeing one of them before her real Valentine arrived. In the seventeenth century, it was apparently usual for married people to have and to be Valentines, as well as young men and maidens. The presents which the women received then were often quite expensive, ranging from embroidered gloves or silk stockings to valuable jewellery among the really well-to-do.

The word ' Valentine ' had a double meaning. Really, it meant the person concerned, the chosen sweetheart, but it was also applied to the Valentine gift and later, when the elaborate present went out of fashion, to the Valentine card which replaced it. The children who used to go round early on the morning of 14 February, looking for gifts from the kind-hearted, had a song which included both meanings. It ran,

Good morrow, Valentine,
Please to give me a Valentine;
I'll be yours if you'll be mine.
Good morrow, Valentine.

Another version of the song said,

Good morrow, Valentine,
Change your luck and I'll change mine.
We are raggety, you are fine,
So pray give us a Valentine.

The singers were usually rewarded with a few coppers, or with cakes, sweets, or oranges.

The substitute for the Valentine gift was the Valentine card, at first handmade, with a verse written on coloured paper, or a drawing of hearts or flowers, and later, the printed card with lace edges, ornaments made of ribbons or feathers, gilded paper, and rhyming mottoes. In the nineteenth century, cards of this kind were sent out by hand or by post in ever-increasing numbers every year, rising to about a million and a half in the 1880s. Thereafter they declined sharply in popularity, and eventually vanished almost completely. In the 1930s, however, they began to be mildly fashionable again, and now, though they will probably never again be so popular as they were a hundred years ago, they can be, and frequently are, bought by the romantic in any stationer's shop.

The Blessing of the Salmon-Net Fisheries on the river Tweed has nothing to do with St Valentine, though it takes place on his feast day. A little before midnight on that anniversary, the Vicar of Norham-on-Tweed conducts an open-air service at the ancient fishery of Pedwell, in which he blesses the river, the 38 salmon-net fisheries on it, the boats and nets, and all the fishermen and others connected with the industry. People come from both sides of the Border and stand round in the February night, often in very wild and stormy weather. This is the opening ceremony of the fishing season, and ends in time for the first boat of the season to start out immediately after midnight.

# 3 Shrovetide and Lent

SHROVE TUESDAY IS THE EVE OF LENT, the 'last day of Shraft', the end of the short festival season which includes Egg Saturday, Quinquagesima Sunday, and Shrove, or Collop, Monday. In some European countries, it is the end of Carnival, that wild and splendid time of pre-Lent rejoicing which undoubtedly began long before Lent was ever thought of, or observed, and which never seems to have flourished in England as it did, and still does, on the Continent. The English name 'Shrove' is derived from the pre-Reformation practice of going to be shriven on that day in preparation for the once severe fast of Lent. What we now call the Pancake Bell (or in some areas, the Fritter, or Guttit, Bell), which, where it is still rung, is supposed to be a signal to start making pancakes, was originally rung to call the faithful to church to make their confessions. But though the religious side of Shrovetide was always important, it was also a time of high festivity, renowned everywhere for the playing of traditional games, cock-fighting, wrestling, dancing, feasting upon pancakes and other good things that the coming 40-day fast would soon forbid, pranks and mischief, and revelries of every kind.

Some of the gaieties still survive in a mild form. Some, happily, do not. Cock-fighting is now illegal, and the barbarous, though once very popular, pastimes of throwing at cocks or ' thrashing the fat hen' have vanished. But pancackes still appear on most family tables, though the housewives who make them are no longer concerned to use up all their remaining fats and butter before Lent begins. At Olney, in Buckinghamshire, a Pancake Race is run annually, and is traditionally said to have been run there on the same date, with occasional lapses, since 1445. However that may be, it was certainly revived in 1948 after one such lapse of many years, and has continued ever since. The competitors, who must be local housewives, assemble in the village square, each one carrying a frying-pan with a cooked pancake in it. At the sound of the Pancake Bell they all start running towards the church, tossing the pancakes three times on the way. If one falls to the ground, as some inevitably do, its owner simply picks it up and tosses it again. The vicar awaits the breathless runners at the church door, and awards the prize of a prayer book to the winner and the runner-up. The verger, who stands behind him, has the right to claim a kiss from the winner, and is usually presented with her pancake as well. The pans are then laid round the font inside the church, and a short service of blessing is held.

Pancake races exist in other English townships, and also, since 1950, at Liberal, in Kansas, USA, but most of those have come into being comparatively recently, and Olney's race is the only one which can be described as genuinely old.

Westminster School has its own special Shrovetide ceremony – the celebrated Pancake Greeze. At eleven o'clock on the Tuesday morning, there enters the Great Schoolroom, first a verger, bearing a silver-topped mace, and then the school cook, wearing his white jacket, cap and apron, and carrying a pancake in a frying-pan. This pancake he tosses over the high iron bar which separates the two halves of the room, and the boys assembled on the other side of the bar scramble for it as it falls. At one time, all the boys of the school took part in the scrimmage, but now each form elects its own representatives. Even so, the struggle is lively enough. The boy who secures the cake, or the largest part of it, receives a guinea from the dean, and the cook, who has done all the skilled work, including the far from easy task of tossing a pancake neatly over a bar 16ft from the ground, receives double that amount.

One of the traditional sports of Shrovetide was football – not the organized game we know today, but the old wild type of game, without proper rules or set teams, played in the streets or in the churchyard, or on any other handy space, and usually, during most of its history, strongly disliked by the authorities because of it rowdiness and the damage done to property. Ball games of a turbulent nature were, and still are, played in many places at certain fixed seasons of the year, including Christmas and Easter, but in the case of football, Shrove Tuesday seems always to have been the favourite day. Chester had a famous street game on that anniversary once. It was, apparently, the custom, ' time out of memory of man ', for the Shoemakers' Company to present a foot-ball valued at 3s 4d to the Drapers' Company, and afterwards for a boisterous game to be played through the city streets, from the Cross on the Roodee (where the presentation ceremony took place, in the presence of the mayor), up to the Common Hall. But that was a long time ago; in 1539, the sport was abolished because of the many injuries sustained by players and spectators alike, and foot races were substituted for it.

Derby had a very violent traditional game, which was played every year between the men of St Peter's and All Saints parishes. The ball was thrown from the Town Hall at noon, or thereabouts, and from then on the game raged up and down between the two goals at opposite ends of the town. Partisan feeling ran very high, and in its last years especially, the game was more like a fierce fight between two parts of the borough than anything else. It was, however, immensely popular; and when, in 1846, it was finally put down, two troops of dragoons had to be brought into the town, many special constables appointed, and the Riot Act read, before the ban could be enforced. At Kingston-on-Thames, and at Dorking, lively games were played along streets lined with barricaded windows until they, too, were finally suppressed, the first in 1866, and the second at the extreme end of the nineteenth century. In Co. Durham, a similar contest at Chester-le-Street, between the Up-streeters and the Down-streeters, survived until 1932.

Shrovetide football is still played at Sedgefield, also in Co. Durham, at Alnwick in Northumberland, Ashbourne in Derbyshire, and at Atherstone in Warwickshire. There is also a traditional game at Workington in Cumberland, but this is played at Easter, one game on Good Friday, the next on Easter Tuesday, and the third on Easter Saturday. The Sedgefield contest, between farmers and tradesmen, is started by the church verger, who passes the ball three times through a bull-ring on the village green, and then throws it to the waiting players. The goals here are a pond and a stream, about 500 yards apart. At Ashbourne, the two old mills which act as goals are three miles apart, and separated by the Henmore Brook and some lesser streams, over or through which the players have to struggle during the course of this strenuous and muddy game. The teams are known as the Up'ards or Down'ards, according to whether the men concerned live north or south of the Henmore. The game is played on Ash Wednesday as well as on Shrove Tuesday, and lasts on both days from two o'clock in the afternoon until ten o'clock at night.

At Atherstone, there are no goals and no teams, each man playing on his own and hoping to win the ball for himself at the end of the game. Once there was an inter-county match between teams from Warwickshire and Leicestershire, but now it has become mainly a contest for individuals, or for gangs. It is played along that part of Watling Street which forms part of the main street of the village and also, south of the township, the boundary between the two counties already mentioned. The ball, adorned with red, white and blue ribbons, and filled with water to prevent it from being kicked too far at once, is thrown from the upper windows of an inn at three o'clock, and kept in play until five o'clock, after which any player who manages to seize it and smuggle it away becomes its owner and the winner of the game.

Alnwick's game is now played in a field called The Pasture, though it was once a street contest like the rest. The teams consist of men from St Michael's and St Paul's parishes; the two goals in the field stand about a quarter of a mile apart, and are decorated with evergreens. On the day of the match, the ball is fetched from Alnwick Castle and ceremonially piped to the field by the Duke of Northumberland's piper. When three goals have been won, the game ends, and a struggle begins to get the ball off the field and over the Duke's boundaries once more. Whoever succeeds in doing this wins a prize.

The Ancient Company of Marblers hold their court at Corfe Castle, in Dorset, on Shrove Tuesday. At this court, new appren-

tices are admitted, and the Warden receives from them traditional gifts of bread, beer and 6s 8d. When the meeting is over,
the quarrymen kick a football along the old road to Poole. This
is not a game in the ordinary sense, but a custom carefully kept
up to maintain an ancient right of way to the Owre Quay at
Poole, whence their stone used to be shipped.

Hurling takes the place of football at St Ives and St Columb
Major in Cornwall. This was formerly an extremely popular
Cornish game, played both as an ordinary pastime, and as an
inter-parish contest. The ball used was, and still is, about the size
of a cricket ball, made of light wood or cork, and thinly coated
with silver. At the beginning of the match, it was thrown up in
the air, and then hurled, tossed, hustled, and carried along
by the players, but never kicked. Richard Carew described it in
his *Survey of Cornwall* (1602) as a very rough game, and no
doubt it was when he wrote about it in the seventeenth century,
and for many years afterwards. ' The hurlers ', he says, ' take their
next way over hills, dales, ditches; yea, and thorow bushes, briars,
mires, plashes, and rivers whatsoever, so as you shall sometimes
see twenty or thirty lie tugging together in the water, scrambling
and scratching for the ball.' As with all these wild games, many
players were injured, and a good deal of damage to property was
done, but its popularity was immense, and it was not until the
late eighteenth or early nineteenth century that first the inter-
parish contest and then the games between different sections of one
community began to die out.

It still survives at St Ives and at St Columb Major, and
occasionally at Bodmin, during the course of bound-beating there.
At St Columb it is played on Shrove Tuesday through the streets
of the town. At St Ives it takes place on the previous day, that is,
on Quinquagesima Monday, locally known as Feasten Monday.
Quinquagesima Sunday is the patronal festival of the parish.
Legend says it was on that day that St Ia, the patron saint of the
town, first landed in Cornwall, after sailing miraculously across
the sea from Ireland on a leaf. Originally this game, like that at
St Columb, was played in the streets, but eventually it was transferred to the beach. The mayor, standing on the West Pier, opened
the proceedings by throwing the silver ball to the people assembled
on the shore below. In 1939, however, the game was once more
transferred, this time to a public park, where it is still played.

Scarborough's special Shrove Tuesday pastime is skipping on

the foreshore. The Pancake Bell, which now lives in the town museum instead of in the parish church, is rung at noon. At about two o'clock, or a little later, people of all sorts begin to drift down to the foreshore, carrying ropes of various thicknesses. Small children come with their mothers, bringing ropes suited to their age; older children, and young lads, arrive singly, or in gangs, hefty fishermen come with stout ropes from their boats. All fall to skipping, alone, or in bands of six or eight or ten, until about tea-time when, gradually, the whirring ropes slacken and stop, and all the people go home again. Motorists have to make their way as best they can through the skipping throng, and mostly they are let through (the ambulance always) with little delay; but if they are unpleasant or awkward, as motorists some-times are when confronted by a hold-up whose cause they do not understand, they are liable to have their cars rocked by the crowd. Of recent years, the police have closed the foreshore to all but essential traffic while the skipping goes on, thereby con-firming the skippers' right to maintain their cherished Shrovetide custom.

No so long ago, children used to go Shroving, or Lent-crocking on Shrove Tuesday (or the night before), and in a few places they still do. They went round in little bands, knocking on house doors, and singing,

> We be come a-shroving,
> For a piece of pancake,
> Or a bite of bacon,
> Or a little truckle cheese
> Of your own making

or, on Shrove Monday,

> Once, twice, thrice,
> I give thee warning,
> Please to make some pancakes,
> 'Gin tomorrow morning,

or some other version of the old begging ditty. Often they took with them a good supply of broken crockery, or stone, with which to bombard the doors of the niggardly. They sang, loudly,

Tippy tippy toe,
Please to give me a pancake,
Or I'll let go!

or, more threateningly,

Here I come, I never came before,
If you don't give me a pancake,
I'll break down your door!

and then, if an ungenerous householder made it necessary (and
sometimes without waiting to see if it was necessary or not), they
hurled their shards against the door with the utmost enthusiasm.

In some parishes, the old Shroving custom has been preserved
by the intervention of adults. At Gittisham, in Devon, where it is
known as Tip-toeing, there is now no village school, and the
children have to go by bus to other schools, where a Shrove
Tuesday half-holiday is not granted, as it used to be at Gittisham.
Only the evening, after their return, remains for Tip-toeing, and
this is now carefully organized by the local Women's Institute.
The children are provided with tea and buns, and are then sent
off to parade the village as of old, singing and visiting all the
houses, and receiving gifts from the inmates. It need hardly
be said that they do not throw stones or crockery at the doors
during this polite and charming ceremony, but this was never a
universal custom, and there does not seem to be any record that it
ever obtained in Gittisham. At Durweston, in Dorset, Mr Valentine Rickman, an inhabitant of the village who died in 1925, left
a sum of £50, vested in the rector and churchwardens, in order to
maintain the ancient custom of Shroving in the parish. The interest
on this sum is divided among all the local schoolchildren who go
Lent-crocking, or Shroving, to at least three houses.

Shrove Tuesday was one of the traditional days on which
in some old-established schools, the custom of barring-out the
schoolmaster was observed. The children locked the master out
of his own school, and bargained with him for a holiday that day,
or sometimes for a series of holidays in the coming terms. If he
managed to force an entry, the victory was his; no holiday was
granted, and he could inflict whatever heavy task he chose upon
his defeated scholars. But if the children could hold out for the
day (or, according to Brand in his *Popular Antiquities*, for three

days), he had to make an agreement with them, and grant at least some of their demands. At Tideswell, in Derbyshire, the custom was kept up until at least as late as 1938. The children went to school riding on long poles and taking it in turns to carry each other, rushed all together into the school, locked the doors before the headmaster could get in, and loudly demanded a holiday in exchange for admission. As, however, Shrove Tuesday was already a holiday in the district, it is clear that the true point of the custom had by then been lost, and that all that remained of it was a Shrovetide frolic. Barring-out was once a widespread schoolboys' custom, not confined to Shrove Tuesday; other traditional occasions for it, varying according to district, were St Andrew's Day, or St Nicholas's Day, the beginning of Harvest, St Thomas's Day, the last day of the Christmas term, or just before Easter.

On Ash Wednesday, Lent begins, and from then on there is no true festival date until Mid-Lent Sunday, the fourth in Lent, better known in England as Mothering Sunday. In pre-Reformation times, this must have been a most welcome relaxation in the midst of the long, harsh fast, when feasting and sports were temporarily restored, and devout men and women from all over the wide parishes of those days came to the Mother Church to make their offerings and meet each other. From at least as far back as the seventeenth century, and probably earlier, it has been a festival marked by small and happy family reunions. Absent children returned home; servants and apprentices were given time off to ' go a-mothering '. They took with them some small gift for their mothers, traditionally a posy of violets or primroses, or a simnel cake, both of which are customary presents for the occasion still.

After the Reformation, the ceremonial visit to the Mother Church of the parish died away, but the domestic custom continued until towards the end of the nineteenth century, when it began to decline. In our own day, it has revived once more and now it is quite usual for family gatherings to be held on that day, and for mothers to receive gifts of various kind from their children. Indeed, the festival has become somewhat over-commercialized, as shopkeepers and others have seized upon it as yet another present-giving anniversary. They also, very deplorably, tend to advertise their wares as ' Mother's Day Gifts ', thereby confusing our ancient Mothering Sunday with the American Mother's Day, which has a totally different history, and falls in a different season. It was invented by Miss Anna Jarvis, of Philadelphia, in 1907, and in 1914 appointed by Congress to be held annually on the second Sunday in May. It is a purely secular occasion, and has no connection with our Mothering Sunday, of which anniversary Miss Jarvis seems never to have heard.

One name for Mid-Lent Sunday is Simnel Sunday because simnel cakes are customarily eaten then. The simnel is a very old cake, of which we hear as far back as 1042 in the *Annals of the Church of Winchester* for that year. Attempts to explain the name account for legends about a mythical couple called Simon and Nell, or cakes made by Lambert Simnel's father and nicknamed after his son when the latter's rebellion failed; but in fact, the word is almost certainly derived from the Latin, *simila*, meaning fine wheaten flour. There are three principal types of simnel cake, named after the towns which first made them. One is the rich, dark Shrewsbury simnel, with its crown of almond paste. Another is the star-shaped Devizes cake, which has no crown, and the third is the famous Bury simnel, flat in shape and filled with currants, almonds, spices, and candied peel. Both in Bury and Devizes, enormous quantities of the traditional cakes are made every year, the work beginning soon after Christmas so that men from both towns who have emigrated and now live abroad may be sure of receiving them in time for Simnel Sunday.

On Palm Sunday, a fortnight later, palms are carried in procession in the churches in memory of Christ's triumphant entry into Jerusalem. Until well towards the end of last century, young people used to ' go a-palming ' in the woods during the three or four days before the festival. They brought back great branches of greenery, for the adornment of the parish church and their own houses; and since there are no palms in England, what they brought was mainly *Salix caprea*, the sallow willow, with its lovely, fluffy, golden catkins, which is sometimes known as the ' English Palm '. On this Sunday also, figs used to be a customary food, either in the form of pies or puddings, or as uncooked fruit. Grocers normally sold immense quantities of figs in preparation for the feast, and in some parts of England, the day itself was known as Fig Sunday. By about 1907, however, the custom began to die out, and today it is quite obsolete.

Many people still alive, whose childhood was spent in the Midlands or in parts of Yorkshire, can remember the old ' Spanish Sunday ' ritual on Palm Sunday. Until as recently as the first quarter of the present century, children in those districts used to put broken pieces of Spanish liquorice, lemon or peppermint sweets, and brown sugar into 12oz glass bottles on the Saturday night, and add a very little tap water, to soften the mixture overnight. In the morning, they all took their bottles to some local well which was always used for the ceremony – usually a holy well of some kind, but sometimes a wishing-well. Round this, they solemnly walked, once, or three times, according to the custom of the district, and then the bottles were filled with well water, and vigorously shaken. The resulting sweet concoction was invariably considered a splendid drink by all the young makers.

At Castleton and Bradwell, in Derbyshire, the pattern was a little different. The children took their bottles to the Lady Wells at Castleton and Great Hucklow on Easter Monday, instead of Palm Sunday; but on the earlier date, they went to the wells and dropped straight new pins into the water. This they did because they believed that if they omitted this part of the ritual, their Easter Monday bottles would break when they went to fill them, and moreover, the ' Lady of the Well ' would not let them have clean water during the coming year.

In Herefordshire, the parishioners of Sellack and King's Caple, and until recently, of Hentland also, remember the charitable bequest of Lady Scudamore who, in or about 1570, charged the revenues of Baysham Court with the provision of cakes and ale, to be served and eaten in the church on Palm Sunday. Her object in doing this was to promote peace and friendship in the three villages, believing, as she did, that those who had shared a common meal on the Sunday before Easter would be willing to compose any differences that might exist between them, and would come together in charity to make their Easter Communion. The original bequest provided for a large cake which the parishioners shared, saying ' God and Good Neighbourhood ' as they did so, and also for glasses of ale. About the middle of the nineteenth century, the funds for the ale seem to have disappeared, and for a time at least, local farmers brought their own ale and cider to the service. In due course, this practice ceased. The large cake was also replaced by small ones, which the churchwardens carried round, immediately after the collection, in baskets covered by white cloths. Now, cakes are no longer used, and instead there are small flat wafers, stamped with the figure of the Paschal Lamb, and known as Pax Cakes. These are not eaten in church, as the cakes that preceded them were, but are handed out by the Vicar, one to each person, as he or she comes out of the building. As he does this, the clergyman greets each one with the old, familiar words, ' God and Good Neighbourhood '.

On Maundy Thursday, the Queen, or in her absence, the Lord High Almoner acting for her, presents the Royal Maundy gifts to as many poor men and as many poor women as there are years in her age. This distribution now usually takes place in Westminster Abbey when the date of the year is even, and in some other great cathedral when it is odd. At one time, the service included the ceremonial washing of the feet of those concerned by the sovereign or his deputy, but since the late seventeenth century, this part of the ritual has been omitted.

Maundy Thursday is the day on which the Last Supper eaten by Christ and His Apostles is commemorated. The name ' maundy ' is said to be derived from *mandatum*, a command, referring to the new commandment of love which Our Lord laid upon the Apostles then. It was on this occasion that He washed their feet, and exhorted them that, as He had done for them, so ought they to do for one another. In the early years of the Church, it was a pious custom for priests and devout people to mark the day by washing the feet of 12 poor men as a sign of Christian humility. In due course, it became usual to add gifts of money, food, or clothing to the foot-washing rite. Gradually, as the years passed, what had originally been a very simple ceremony developed into something splendid and colourful, in which the kings of a number of European countries, great nobles, and high dignitaries of the Church all played their part. How soon the symbolical 12 poor men changed to as many as there were years in the donor's age is uncertain; but it is recorded that in 1212, when King John had reigned for 13 years, he gave 13d each to 13 men at Rochester, and that in 1361, Edward III, being then 50 years old, washed the feet of 50 poor men, and gave away 50 pairs of slippers.

Formerly, food, wine, clothes, or the material for making them, and other miscellaneous gifts were included in the Royal Maundy, as custom, or the generosity of the giver dictated. At one time, it was usual for the sovereign to present the robe that he or she wore during the ceremony, as Mary I certainly did in 1556, for we hear of her giving her Maundy robe of purple cloth, lined with marten's fur. Queen Elizabeth, however, in 1572, redeemed her garment by the payment of 20s to each of the poor people present.

This sum, paid ' for the redemption of Her Majestie's gown ', is still given today. So also are certain other money allowances which, in the course of time, have replaced, first the women's clothes, then the provisions, and finally the cloth for the men's garments.

James II was the last English king to perform the feet-washing rite in person. This he did in 1685, and from then on, it was performed by the Lord High Almoner until about the middle of the eighteenth century, when it was abolished. The distribution of the Royal Maundy went on without a break, though it was not made again by any reigning monarch until 1923, when George V presented his own gifts, 247 years after King James. Edward VIII and George VI did the same in their turn, the former once and the latter seven times, and since her accession, Queen Elizabeth II has rarely missed ' making her maunds ' in person.

The modern ceremony consists of a lovely and colourful procession, prayers, hymns and anthems, the distribution of the Maundy Money and the other sums due, and the final Blessing and singing of the National Anthem. The Queen's Bodyguard of the Yeoman of the Guard are present at the ceremony, and two of them carry a great gold dish, on which the various purses with their thongs of different colours hanging over the edge are piled. The Queen (or her deputy) passes down the waiting line of men and women twice, distributing to each one, first the purse containing the redemption money for the clothing, and then, during the second distribution, the fee for the provisions, and the Maundy Money itself. The last consists of a silver penny, twopenny, threepenny, and fourpenny pieces, specially minted for the occasion, and corresponding in number to the Queen's age. They are legal tender, and can be kept or spent by the recipient, as he or she wishes. Mostly, of course, they are kept as cherished treasures, and it is only the larger sum derived from the various allowances which is spent, as a very welcome addition to an Old Age Pension.

On Good Friday, countrymen plant potatoes and sow parsley, Sussex people skip, the children in the South End of Liverpool ' burn Judas ', and everyone eats Hot Cross buns. In Brighton, formerly, the day was known as Long Rope Day, because then the fishermen and their families skipped on the beach and in the Fish Market, and in the open streets. This custom began to die out in the first years of the present century, and ceased altogether when the beaches were closed during World War II. Skipping,

D

however, still goes on at Alciston, and so, since 1954, it does at South Heighton, near Newhaven. Until very recently, there was skipping on Good Friday on Parker's Piece, in Cambridge, as formerly there was by the Bartlow Hills, on the border between Cambridgeshire and Essex. Both these customs have now vanished. Marbles was another popular pastime associated with Good Friday, especially in Surrey and Sussex, where the anniversary was some times called Marbles Day, because it marked the end of the very short marbles season. This ran only from Ash Wednesday to Good Friday, and ended precisely at noon on the latter day. Men played the game very seriously all through Lent, ending as a rule with a championship match on Good Friday morning. A survival of this is the well-known match at Tinsley Green, near Crawley, which is said to have been played on the same site and according to the same rules, including that of ending at noon, since the beginning of the seventeenth century.

In the South End of Liverpool, near the docks (but not, apparently, in any other part of the city), small bands of children set out very early on Good Friday morning, each little group carrying with it a straw-stuffed effigy which is known as Judas. At sunrise, the leader hoists this figure on a pole and knocks with it on the upper windows of the local houses, while all the other children shout, ' Judas is short of a penny for his breakfast!' The desired money having been supplied by the householders, who know they will not get any peace until it is given, the young people then proceed to ' burn Judas ' ceremonially. They make a fire in the middle of the street, using the wood, straw, and other materials they have been collecting for some time. The effigy is thrown on it, and round it they all dance, shouting, and heaping more fuel on the flames. Other groups, meantime, are doing the same elsewhere, and before long, the police begin to be active. A policeman arrives suddenly, scatters the fire, and bears off the effigy to the police station, followed, of course, by the loudly protesting children. Tradition says that, even without the interference of the police, the burning must take place by eleven o'clock in the morning, and that by noon, all fires must be out, and all the young ritualists off the streets.

This curious custom is said to have sprung from memories of the Spanish sailing ships which once came to the nearby docks with fruit and wine. In Spain, Portugal, and Latin America, it was a widespread practice to beat, hang, or burn effigies of Judas on

Good Friday, and this ritual was carried through by sailors on board ship, in whatever port they found themselves when the day came round. The idea of punishing Judas is not, of course, confined to Spain and Portugal. In Devonshire, formerly, it was considered lucky to break a piece of pottery on Good Friday, because the sharp edges were supposed to pierce the body of Judas. In Corfu, it was customary to hurl crockery down a steep hill, while calling down curses upon him by name. The straw figure known as Jack-o'-Lent, once dragged about English parishes on Ash Wednesday, pelted with stones, abused and derided, and finally shot to pieces, or burnt, either on the same day, or on Palm Sunday, was often supposed to represent Judas Iscariot; but it is perhaps more likely that it was, at least originally, the hated figure of Winter, and that its noisy destruction was a relic of the ancient ceremony of Driving Out Winter.

On Good Friday, most people eat hot cross buns for breakfast. These small, round, spiced cakes, marked with a cross, appear to be the Christian descendants of the cross-marked wheaten cakes which the Pagan Greeks and Romans ate at the Springtime festival of Diana, and of those others, also cross-marked, which the pre-Christian Saxons feasted upon round about the Vernal Equinox. In the eighteenth and nineteenth centuries, hot cross buns were always made on the day of eating, by housewives who rose very early for the purpose, or by bakers who worked during the night to have them ready for the breakfast tables of their customers. Men used to go about the early morning streets of towns, carrying trays full of steaming buns covered by a cloth, and crying,

> Hot Cross Buns!
> One-a-penny, two-a-penny,
> Hot Cross Buns!

Now, however, this cheerful sound has gone from our streets. Bakers no longer work at night, and as far as home cooking is concerned, far fewer housewives trouble to rise so early in order to bake their own buns. The buns we now eat on Good Friday morning are, deplorably, nearly always bought on the previous day, and need no more attention than simple reheating.

An old and once widespread belief was that the true Good Friday buns – that is, those made in the old manner on the day itself – would never go mouldy and, if kept, could be used to cure a variety of ailments, such as diarrhoea, dysentery, whooping-cough, and the tiresome affliction known as ' summer sickness '. They were also supposed to protect the house that contained them from fire, the granary from rats and, when taken on board ship by a member of the crew, to avert shipwreck. The same magical properties were ascribed to bread baked on Good Friday; but needless to say, the Thursday-made bread and buns of modern usage have no such virtues.

Many popular superstitions were once associated with Good Friday. Most of them are forgotten now, but traces of a few still linger on in some districts. Blacksmiths, formerly, would not shoe a horse on that day because of the terrible use to which nails had been put, long ago, on Calvary. Miners would not go down the pit, believing that some disaster would occur underground if they did so. Housewives would not sweep their houses on this anniversary (any more than they would on New Year's Day), because to do so was to sweep away the life of one of the family, most likely its head. Similarly, it was very unlucky to wash clothes or linen. The water would be found tinged with blood, or the clothes on the line spotted with it; in Worcestershire, within the last ten years or so, it was said that, even if no washing was actually done, soapsuds must not be left in the boiler over Good Friday, or a death would follow.

A curious belief of another type is contained in the old rhyme which runs,

> If Our Lord falls in Our Lady's lap,
> England will meet with a great mishap.

This refers to the date of the month on which Good Friday or Easter Sunday may happen to fall. An ancient tradition says that the Crucifixion took place on 25 March (now Lady Day), and that if either the Friday or the Sunday coincide with this date (which can only happen in the case of a very early Easter), the omen is bad. This rhyming prophecy has been quoted, with serious mean-ing at least twice in the present century, after the deaths of two well-loved kings. In 1910, Good Friday fell on 25 March, and in the following May, Edward VII died after a brief illness; in 1951, Easter Sunday coincided with Lady Day, and nearly eleven months later, George VI died suddenly on 6 February 1952.

# 4 Eastertide

EASTER DAY, the Feast of the Resurrection of Our Lord, is the greatest of the Christian festivals, and almost certainly the one which has been observed longest. Although we cannot now name the exact date on which the first Easter fell, we can be sure that there has never, from the very beginning, been a year in which its anniversary was not joyously honoured, at first by those who remembered the original day of wonder and happiness beyond hope, and later by those to whom they handed on the good news. In the early years, it was not kept on the same day everywhere, but after many years of controversy, it was decided at the Council of Nicaea in AD 325 (and finally confirmed in the sixth century) that Easter should be kept on the Sunday following the first full moon after, or on, the Vernal Equinox, but if that moon happened to be full on a Sunday, then Easter should be the Sunday after. The Vernal Equinox was assumed to occur on 21 March. Because of this decision, the festival can never fall earlier than 22 March, or later than 25 April, but within those limits, it remains a

movable feast, in spite of the efforts of some to whom convenience is all to fix it for good and all on one of the Sundays in
April.

Easter also has its pagan associations because it came in the
Spring, and coincided in time with some of the cherished vernal
festivals of heathendom. St Bede tells us that our English name
for it was derived from Eostre, the North European Goddess of
Spring and of the Dawn, after whom the early Anglo-Saxons
called the month of April *Eosturmonath*. The animal most sacred
to her worship was the hare, that swift and fascinating creature
which folk tradition in most European countries has connected
with Easter for centuries.

At Easter all the churches are filled with spring flowers of every
kind. Arum lilies and white narcissi adorn the high altar, with
the dark-green branches of yew which stand for life everlasting,
and in other parts of the church, flowers of all sorts, especially
primroses, fill every corner. On the Vigil of Easter, the lovely
ceremony of making New Fire with flint and steel, in the old
manner takes place in most parishes, together with the lighting
of the Paschal Candle from the new-struck flame, and the blessing
of the Water. One very old custom, which lasted all through the
nineteenth century, and into the twentieth until nearly as late as
the outbreak of World War I, was to go out before sunrise to see
the sun dance as it rose for joy that Our Lord had risen. It was
widely believed that it did so, and people of all ages assembled on
high ground, or climbed to the tops of hills to see this miracle.
Many afterwards asserted that they had seen it. Perhaps they had,
with the eye of faith, or perhaps through that natural flickering
and radiating effect that is sometimes visible in a sunrise viewed
from a high place. That the sun did actually dance on Easter
morning, leaping up and down and changing colour, or – according to other accounts – whirling round like a wheel, was very
genuinely believed all through Great Britain and Ireland, and
failure to see it was often explained by saying that the Devil
commonly tried to put some obstruction in the way of the
observer.

Eggs are the natural symbol of continuing life and resurrection,
and they have been so regarded by men of varying religions for
untold centuries. The early Christians saw them as emblems of
Christ's rising from the grave, and long before that time, they
were an essential part of the Spring Festival celebrations in

many lands. They are still favourite gifts at Eastertide, in England as elsewhere. It is true that nowadays they are often mere imitations of the genuine article, made of chocolate or marzipan, or simply egg-shaped cases of decorated cardboard, into which some small gift is inserted. But the true Easter Egg still exists, at least in houses where the old tradition is remembered. This is a real egg from the poultry-yard, with its shell coloured, of late years with ordinary commercial dyes, but formerly, and occasionally still, with the lovely natural dyes obtained from flowers, leaves, mosses, or wood chips. Spinach or anemone petals for green, gorse blossom for yellow, cochineal for scarlet, logwood for purple can all be used, and much else besides. One of the simplest methods of colouring is to boil the egg with the outer skin of an onion wrapped round it; the result is a shell tinted a delicate mottled yellow, or a pleasant clear brown. Sometimes, if there is anyone with clever fingers in the house, the egg may be adorned with an inscribed motto, or a design of some kind, executed with a wax pencil, or a sharp stylus, or engraving tool.

In northern England, such eggs were, and still are, known as pace eggs. In the three or four days on either side of Easter, young men and boys used to go out pace-egging, collecting eggs for themselves, and acting the Pace Egg Play, which is the Easter version of the ancient Mumming Play. They still do in some regions, only now it is mainly children who go round pace-egging, and the old play, once the essential heart of the custom, is often forgotten. It is still acted in Yorkshire's Calder Valley, by the boys of the Calder High School, and also in a few other northern places; but elsewhere it is usually omitted by the young pace-eggers, who have probably never learnt the words or seen it acted. They often blacken their faces, or wear some fantastic form of dress, as their predecessors did, but otherwise they content themselves with demanding their largesse of eggs (or anything else the householder may give them) through some traditional rhyme, such as,

> Please, Mrs Whiteleg,
> Please to give us an Easter egg.
> If you won't give us an Easter Egg,
> Your hens will all lay addled eggs,
> And your cocks all lay stones.

Egg-rolling is a long-established Easter pastime which still flourishes in many parts of northern England, Scotland, Ulster, and the Isle of Man. Usually on the Bank Holiday Monday, but sometimes on Easter Sunday itself, children and young people gather on some convenient hill or slope, and roll as many hard-boiled, coloured eggs down it as they have been able to collect in the days beforehand. This goes on until the eggs are cracked and battered, after which their owners eat them. Sometimes the sport takes the form of a competitive game, the winner being he or she whose egg survives the longest, but in most places, it is the rolling and eating which provides the fun. Some towns have a traditional egg-rolling site, like the Castle Moat at Penrith, Arthur's Seat at Edinburgh, or the steep grassy slopes of Avenham Park in Preston in Lancashire. In the latter place, it has become customary to roll, and subsequently eat, oranges as well as eggs. This is a purely modern addition to the ritual, which nevertheless adds a golden gaiety to an occasion already made bright by literally thousands of coloured eggs, all rolling and bouncing together downwards to the banks of the river Ribble.

Eostre's hare appears in the folklore of many European countries, including our own. At one time, she was the bringer of Easter eggs, and children of many districts used to search in the garden or the outhouses for the eggs she had hidden there. At Coleshill, in Warwickshire, young men rose early on Easter Monday morning, and set out to run down a hare. If they could catch it, and bring it to the rector before ten o'clock, he was obliged to give them a calf's head and a hundred eggs for their breakfast, and also a groat in money. In Leicester, until about the end of the eighteenth century, there was a Hare Hunt, in which the mayor and the town officers, and a large crowd of citizens all took part. On Easter Monday morning the company rode out to a cave known as Black Annis's Bower, on the nearby Dane Hills. Outside this cave, they all indulged in games and sport until noon, when the Hunt began. This was probably a real hare hunt once, but in the course of time it had degenerated into a drag hunt in which a dead cat soaked in aniseed water was drawn on a zig-zag course down the hillside, excitedly pursued by hounds, horsemen, and foot runners. The Hunt ran from the cave mouth through lanes and alleyways, passages, private gardens, and streets until it ended at the door of the mayor's house in the town. The day ended with a feast given by the mayor to his friends. Exactly when this lively

custom began is unknown, though it is described as ' ancient '
in the town records of 1668. In the late eighteenth century, it
slowly died out, though for some years it was replaced by an
annual gathering, now extinct, known as the Dane Hills Fair.

These two old hare customs have left no active traces today,
but the Hare Pie Scramble at Hallaton (and the Bottle-kicking that
follows it) goes on as vigorously as ever on Easter Monday. At
some unknown date, a piece of land was settled upon the rectors
of this Leicestershire parish on condition that each one in
turn should furnish, every year, at Easter, two hare pies, 24 penny
loaves, and a quantity of ale, the solid food to be scrambled for
on a piece of rising ground called the Hare Pie Bank. Hares were
specially mentioned as the meat for the pies, though they are out
of season at Easter. This, together with the fact that in some
years the figure of a sitting hare on the top of a pole has been
carried in the procession, suggests that here we have traces of
some far older custom connected with the Easter Hare. Nowadays,
the two hare pies have become one large pie, filled with beefsteak
or some other meat, but not with hare meat, and the penny loaves
have disappeared. The pie is cut up by the rector, the pieces are
put into a sack, and are carried in procession to the Hare Pie
Bank, where they are scrambled for with a great deal of laughter
and merriment.

After this comes the Bottle-kicking contest. Three stalwart
young men walk in procession to the Bank, carrying the ' bottles ',
which are really small wooden barrels bound with iron hoops. Of
these, two are filled with ale; the third is a dummy. As soon as the
Hare Pie Scramble is ended, one of the full barrels is put into a
round hollow on the top of the Bank, and the lively game of
Bottle-kicking begins. There are two teams of indeterminate size,
the men of Hallaton, and the men of Medbourne, which is the
next parish. On this occasion, the name ' Medbourne ' is stretched
to cover any person (not a Hallatonian) who cares to take part in
the game. The players' object is to get the barrel away from the
Bank and over the boundary line, into one parish or the other.
One of the full barrels is first fought for, very fiercely, and which-
ever side wins that round claims the ale it contains. The dummy is
then contested, with equal vigour, and the game ends with the
broaching of the second full barrel at the market cross on Hallaton
Green, where its contents are joyfully shared by both sides.

An old Easter Monday custom which survived until almost

the eve of World War II was Riding the Black Lad (or the Black Knight) at Ashton-under-Lyne, in Lancashire. Regularly every year until 1914, and thereafter rather more intermittently until 1938, a cheerful and noisy procession wound its way through Ashton's streets on Easter Monday. Its central feature was the effigy of a knight in black armour and a black velvet cloak, mounted on horseback, and accompanied by a band of young men, some also mounted and some on foot, who were supposed to be the knight's retainers. Crowds of people flocked in every year from the surrounding districts to see the fun, and the procession slowly passed through streets densely packed with shouting and jeering spectators. Eventually it came to an appointed open space, and halted there. Then the black knight's effigy was dismounted, pelted with stones, mud, and anything else that was handy, insulted, execrated, and at the last, shot to pieces with guns.

The Black Lad of this ceremony was popularly supposed to represent Sir Ralph de Assheton, Lord of Middleton, and son (by a second marriage) of Sir John de Assheton, who flourished in the fifteenth century. With his brother, Robin, he held the right of guld-riding in Ashton parish. This meant that he was empowered to inspect certain lands annually, and to fine, or otherwise punish, neglectful husbandmen who allowed carr-gulds (corn-marigolds), and other weeds to grow unchecked upon them. In the manor rental of 1422, it is stated that the two brothers ' have the sour guld rode and stane rynges for the term of their lives ', the 'sour guld ' here mentioned being, apparently, the wet, low-lying lands near the town that were known as the Sour Carrs. Tradition says that Sir Ralph performed his inspector's duties with great and unnecessary severity, and was fiercely hated in consequence. He is often accused of other tyrannies also, but these may well have been mere storyteller's additions to the legend. In the end, he is said to have been murdered by some infuriated person in the open street of the town.

When Sir John de Assheton died, his heir, who was Sir Ralph's half-brother, abolished the guld-riding, to the great joy of the townspeople. He may well have done this, but by an almost incredible addition to the tale, he is also said to have given money for the foundation of an annual celebration whereby the memory of Sir Ralph's hated visits to the Sour Carrs should be kept green in the minds of the people. From this gift, and his encouragement, the ceremony of Riding the Black Lad is supposed to have arisen.

It is, however, difficult to believe that any man should have wished to perpetuate the misdeeds of his own half-brother in this way, even if enmity existed between them, and we do not know that it did. It seems more likely that, because he was hated and feared in his lifetime, Sir Ralph became confused in folk tradition with the age-old figure of Winter which, in many districts (and possibly in Ashton also, though we have no proof of this) used to be ceremonially driven out at, or near, the Spring Festival, carrying with it all the sins and sorrows of the community, and all the cold, hunger, darkness, and misfortunes of the winter that had just ended.

Until about the middle of last century, a custom rather like Ashton's Riding the Black Lad was observed on Easter Monday at Neston in Cheshire. Here, however, there were no well-known names of historical personages from the Middle Ages, and no explanatory legend based upon past events in the history of the parish. A man was hired to ride upon a donkey from one end of Neston's long High Street to the other, between two lines of jeering, cat-calling villagers, who pelted him with mud and clods and rotten eggs as he rode along. At the end of this very unpleasant journey, he dismounted, was paid the sum agreed (enough, one hopes, to make it all worthwhile, but the customary sum does not seem to have been recorded), and simply rode away. This was the end of the odd ritual, which was known as Riding the Lord. In its later years, at least, no one was able to give any account of its meaning or origin, nor any reason why it should be regularly performed at Easter, except that ' it had always been done '. Clearly, the ' Lord ' must have been some sort of scapegoat at one time, but of the custom's beginnings and history, no one seems to have had any knowledge. Now the Lord rides no more, and few people in modern Neston are even aware that he ever did so.

In north-western England, and along the Welsh Border, the old custom of Lifting (or Heaving) at Easter was kept up until about the beginning of the second half of last century. On Easter Monday, the young men of the parish went round to all the village houses, to lift the women, and on Easter Tuesday, the women went round in their turn to lift the men. Each party carried a decorated chair, stoutly built, and adorned with ribbons, flowers, and greenery, and in this the inmates of each house, young and old alike, were made to sit while the lifters hoisted them three times into the air and turned them about. For this, the reward of a small sum of money and, in the case of a pretty girl being lifted, a kiss, could be claimed. In a few parishes, though not very many, the order of visiting was reversed, and it was the women who went out on the first day, and the men on the second. As with many customs of this sort, the proceedings ended exactly at noon.

In the villages, where everybody knew everybody else, Lifting was often a charming and happy ceremony, which was enjoyed by all concerned in it. It has been suggested that its origins lie far back in the past, and are connected with ancient magico-agricultural rites intended to make the crops grow. But in its heyday, few people doubted that the custom began as a purely Christian celebration commemorating Our Lord's Resurrection. F. T. Havergal relates in *Herefordshire Words and Phrases* (1887), that Herefordshire lifters used to sing ' Jesus Christ has risen again!' as they came indoors; there, too, as in Shropshire, the feet of the person lifted were often sprinkled with water from a wet bunch of flowers brought in for the purpose. At Neston, it was usual for the girls to show great fear of the lifters, or to pretend to do so, and to rush indoors when they saw them approaching and bar the doors and windows. It seems, however, that theirs was a ritual rather than an actual fear, and it was understood that if the young men could get in by any window ' accidentally ' left open, or by any other means, get in they would, and duly lift those within.

In the bigger manufacturing towns, Lifting, though it was well known, was not always so pleasant, nor so decorously performed as it was in the country. Respectable young women were careful to stay indoors until after noon had struck, and to keep every door and window genuinely locked against all possible intruders. The ceremonial visits to individual houses were often omitted, and Lifting, with or without a decorated chair, took place in the open streets. Men going about their normal business, or perhaps coming newly to the town from elsewhere, were liable to be seized without warning by five or six brawny young (or middle-aged) women, Lifted, in a chair if one was provided, if not, in the women's arms, and vigorously kissed. They were also expected to reward the Lifters with money on their release. A letter, published in *Adams Weekly Courant* for 26 March 1771, complains bitterly that people coming to Chester for business reasons on Easter Monday were frequently hoisted thus without ceremony and forced to pay ransom several times during the course of the morning. The writer demands that the custom should be put down forthwith by the magistrates, but, then and later, the experience of Manchester, Bolton, Kidderminster, and other towns was to show that this was not quite as easy as it sounded. Baring-Gould, who was himself once roughly lifted by a band of Basque girls when he was in the Pyrenees, records how one of his friends, being in Wednesbury one Easter Monday, was ' lifted and kissed until he was black in the face, by a party of leather-breeched coalpit women '. He also mentions in a footnote in William Henderson's *Folk-Lore of the Northern Counties of England and the Borders* (1866 edition), a rather nervous clergyman, a schoolmaster, who, at Warrington, was set on by a gang of mill-girls, ' heaved ', and paraded in triumph through the streets of the town, notwithstanding his most urgent protests and his unavailing struggles.

In the 1870s, Lifting was already dying out in many districts. In 1883, a man living at Heswall in Cheshire brought an action before the Neston magistrates against three men who had come to his house to Lift his wife. Ten years earlier, such an action would hardly have been conceivable, and even in the 1880s, it showed a singular ignorance of local tradition. The men pleaded old Cheshire custom, as was their right, and the case was dismissed after the payment of costs, and apologies from the defendants.

The second Monday and Tuesday after Easter Day together make up the little season of Hocktide, which was once a lively holiday occasion in many parts of England, but is now actively observed only at Hungerford, in Berkshire. Until about the middle of the seventeenth century, the two days were marked, not only by lively games and merriment, but also by the collection of money in the streets for the church funds. On the Monday (usually, though, as with Lifting, the day order was reversed in some places), the women went out, stopped all the male passers-by they could catch, and demanded ransom from them before they were allowed to proceed. On the Tuesday, the men did the same by all the women they met. At one time, the collectors of both sexes were allowed to bind their victims with ropes, for which reason the Hock days were known as Binding Monday and Tuesday; but after the Reformation, the actual binding of passengers was forbidden, and the ropes were used only for stretching across the roads, and thus barring the way until due payment had

been made. The result of both the women's and the men's
'gaderyngs' was usually a considerable addition to the parish
funds, though it is interesting to note from the churchwardens'
surviving accounts that, all through the centuries, the women
have always been better collectors than the men. 'Now we observe
two hock days,' wrote Dr Plot in his *Natural History of Oxfordshire* (1676), 'on Monday for the women, which is much the
more solemn, and Tuesday for the men, which is very inconsider-
able.'

At Hungerford, Hock Tuesday is the great day of the civic
year. This town, unlike most English boroughs, has no Mayor or
Corporation, but is governed by 12 Feoffees chosen from amongst
the commoners, and a High Constable, Bailiff, Portreeve, Tuttimen, and other officials, who are elected at the court held on Hock
Tuesday. This court meets at nine o'clock in the morning, and an
hour before that time, the long note of a horn, blown by the
Town Crier, reminds the townspeople of their duty to attend it.
The horn now used dates only from 1634, and is a replica
of one much older, which John of Gaunt bestowed upon Hungerford in the fourteenth century, along with certain fishing rights in
the river Kennet, and some manorial privileges. These rights and
privileges still exist, and so does the horn, but the latter is no
longer sounded on Hock Day, as it once was. When the horn-
blowing is over, the Bellman goes through the streets, crying,

Oyez! Oyez! Oyez!

All ye commoners of the Borough and Manor of Hungerford are requested to attend your Court House at the Hall
at nine o'clock this morning to answer your names on penalty
of being fined.

God Save The Queen!

Theoretically at least, every commoner is bound to attend this
court, and also another on the following Friday, when the new
officials are sworn in, or else pay a fine of one penny. This,
obviously, is not a very heavy penalty, but there is also a risk that
those who neither come nor pay may lose their fishing and
common rights for that year.

While the court sits, the Tuttimen, two in number, go on their rounds. Each one carries a tuttipole, a long, beribboned staff, adorned with a gay tutti, or posy, of flowers (from which it gets its name), and surmounted by an orange. With them goes a man wearing a top hat with cock's feathers in it, and carrying a sack of oranges. He is known as the Orange Scrambler. The Tuttimen were originally the Tything men of the borough, whose duty it was to guard and watch over the townsmen and their property during their years of office. They had the right, on Hock Tuesday, to demand a head penny from every commoner in return for these services, and this right still exists, though the duties of their office are not now as strenuous as they were in the past.

Accompanied by the Orange Scrambler, they visit every common-right house in the borough to demand their due pence. Women have the right to pay with a kiss instead of a coin, and this is now the usual custom. When a kiss has been received, an orange from the top of a tuttipole is given, and this is at once replaced by the Orange Scrambler from his sack. All the children in the houses visited are given oranges as well. The Tuttimen also have the right to stop any woman encountered in the street, be she commoner, visitor, or passing motorist, and require from her a coin or a kiss.

After the meeting of the Tuesday Court, there is a civic luncheon, traditionally held at the Three Swans Hotel. The Tuttimen are present at this, and afterwards they and the Orange Scrambler go outside and throw oranges to be scrambled for by a waiting crowd of children. Inside the hotel, the ceremony of Shoeing the Colt takes place. The Constable rises and declares that there are strangers present, and that the Colt must be shod. A man wearing a blacksmith's apron and carrying a hammer then comes in, and with him, another man carrying a box of farrier's nails. The Colt, by which is meant any newcomer or visitor to the town who may be present, is then 'shod' by these two, who pretend to drive nails into the sole of their victim's shoe until he cries 'Punch!' and thereafter pays for a round of drinks. By this ceremony, he ceases to be a stranger or a newcomer, and becomes a true man of Hungerford. He has the right to refuse to play his part in the shoeing, but in that case, he has to pay a fine of £1. It need hardly be said that only very rarely does anyone refuse on so festive an occasion.

The Hocktide ceremonies in Hungerford end with the Friday meeting and the swearing-in of the newly elected officers, after

which the Constable usually gives a dinner at which John of
Gaunt's health is drunk in silence. A civic attendance at the Parish
Church on Sunday brings the celebrations to their end.

# 5 The Month of May

THE ANCIENT CELTIC CALENDAR, which divided the year into
two main seasons, winter and summer, made 1 May the first day
of summer, and therefore an occasion of universal rejoicing. From
time immemorial there have been maypoles and garlands then,
Lords and Ladies, May carols, dancing and hobby-horses and
Jacks-in-the-Green, and a host of other festal customs. Some of
these merriments are still with us though many have vanished,
and others have greatly changed in the course of centuries. Once,
in almost every parish, young men and girls went out into the
open country in the small hours of May morning to ' fetch home
the May '. They gathered boughs of birch and sycamore and hawthorn and every kind of flower, and when the sun had risen
they returned home with armfuls of blossom and greenery, with
which they decorated their houses and their parish church, and
made their garlands. The Puritans of the sixteenth and seventeenth centuries detested this custom, which was already hoary
with age in their day, partly because it was old and gay and rooted

E

in paganism, and partly because they felt that running about together in the pre-dawn darkness put too great a strain on young morals, as indeed, it sometimes did. But they could not suppress it altogether because many of their contemporaries saw no harm in it, and the people loved it. It was not until the beginning of the nineteenth century that the old night-rambling custom finally died away. One verse of a traditional May song, still remembered and sometimes sung, commemorates it, though the children who sing it have quite certainly spent the previous night sleeping peacefully in their beds. It runs:

> We've been rambling all this night,
> And some part of the day,
> And now returning back again,
> We have brought you a branch of May.

May Eve, in some districts, was a time for lively antics of every kind, and was known as Mischief Night, as Hallowe'en, or later, Guy Fawkes' Eve, was elsewhere. Horns were very favourite instruments at this season once, and every young lad took care to provide himself in good time with a tin trumpet, or a cow horn. Little gangs of boys went about blowing such horns during most of the day, beginning at daybreak, or sometimes even earlier; in seventeenth-century Oxford, according to John Aubrey in *Remaines of Gentilisme and Judaisme, 1686–7* (ed. J. Britten, 1881) 'the boys do blow Cow horns and hollow Caxes all night'. In the north-western and midland counties, the May Birchers used to go round the parish on May Eve, silently and unseen, to leave their secret tokens outside the sleeping houses during the hours of darkness. They took with them branches of greenery, or flower sprigs, each one carefully chosen because its name rhymed with whatever quality they considered the most outstanding in the householder they intended to visit, or in some member of his family. These they set against or over the house door, to be found in the morning.

Hawthorn in blossom was always a compliment, and so was pear, which rhymes with fair of face or character, and lime, which rhymes with prime. So too, the rowan, commonly called wicken, which rhymes with chicken, and was a term of endearment. But thorn (other than the flowering hawthorn) meant that someone in the house was an object of scorn, a briar that he (or she) was a liar, a nut branch that the woman of the house was a slut, and so on through a long range of clearly understood symbols. Nettles, elders, thistles, and weeds needed no rhyming associations to convey their message of insult. This curious custom survived in the places where it was known until nearly the end of the last century, and then slowly died away as villages became larger and communities less closely knit.

The age-old custom of ' washing in the dew ' still lingers in many country districts, though it is much less usual now than it used to be. Girls everywhere believed, as some still do, that to rise before dawn on May morning and wash their faces in dew gathered from the grass will not only bring them good luck, but will make them beautiful. At one time, it was generally believed that May dew was a cure for consumption and goitres and some other ills, but no one seems to remember this now. It is still, however, used by some girls to do away with freckles and other skin blemishes.

At six o'clock in May morning (five o'clock formerly, before the introduction of Summer Time), the choristers of Magdalen College, Oxford, go up to the top of the Tower and sing the Latin hymn, *Te Deum Patrem colimus*. A considerable crowd always gathers to hear them do this, even at that early hour, and the bridge below the Tower and the beginning of the High Street are usually tightly wedged with people. When the singing is over, the bells in the Tower are pealed, and then the Morris dancers – the old Headington Quarry team and the newer Morris Men from Oxford – set off through the streets, and dance in five or six recognized places.

Various suggestions have been put forward to account for the origin of this custom. The most probable seems to be that it began as a ceremony held on the completion of the Tower in 1509. Anthony Wood, writing in the seventeenth century, says that the choristers, ' according to an ancient custom', gave a kind of secular concert, ' to salute Flora ', at four o'clock on May morning. The substitution of the present hymn for more varied music did not take place until the eighteenth century and was largely due to our uncertain English weather. On an exceedingly wet May Day, the singers were so late in getting to the Tower that there was no time to perform the music arranged for them. They therefore hastily substituted *Te Deum Patrem colimus*, for the simple reason that they all knew it by heart. It had long been part of the College

Grace; and from then on, it became the Hymn traditionally sung
on May Morning.

At Southampton, a somewhat similar ceremony takes place on
May Day on the top of Bargate, or rather, it did, until the old
gate became unsafe, and it was no longer possible to use the top
as a singing platform. The custom therefore lapsed for some time,
but since 1957 it has been revived in a slightly modified form.
Hymns are now sung at sunrise on May morning by the choristers
of King Edward VI School, not on Bargate itself, but on the lawn
next to it.

The May Garland is a summer emblem of very great antiquity,
which has given to May Day the secondary name of Garland
Day. It has always varied considerably in form and shape, ranging from a simple bunch of flowers tied to the top of a long staff,
or a pole wreathed with flowers, to the elaborate double-hoop
garland, densely covered with spring flowers of every kind, or the
less usual pyramid, also thickly covered by blossoms, and usually
very tall, often rising to a height of 5 or 6ft. Sometimes there is a
May Doll, seated in the centre of a hoop garland, or fixed upon
the front of a pyramid. These May Dolls, which are usually quite
ordinary girl dolls, dressed in white, and occasionally veiled,
almost certainly meant the visible summer once, but now, where
they still exist, they are more often explained by the young
garland-bearers as representing the Virgin Mary, or a goddess, or
the May Queen. At Bampton, in Oxfordshire, for instance, where
a number of doll-bearing garlands are still brought out every year,
an enquirer not long since was told by one of the young people
concerned that the doll in their garland was Minerva.

The hoop garland is made upon a framework of two or more
intersecting hoops, upon which the flowers are piled. A flower
crown can be constructed from wooden or wire half-hoops set
on a circular base; a pyramid is built up on parallel hoops kept in
place by upright poles. Simpler than any of these is the cross
garland, which is a plain wooden cross, varying in size according
to local custom, and very easy to make and cover with flowers.
In Oxford, after the May-singing is over, small bands of children
can often be seen in the streets carrying such crosses. These, unlike
most floral garlands found elsewhere, almost always display
quantities of cuckoo flowers along with the rest. An old and
strict tradition says that these flowers are unlucky in a garland,
so much so that if some sprigs are included by mistake, the whole

garland must be undone and made up again from the beginning. Whether anyone really believes this superstition today is questionable, but it is a fact that cuckoo flowers are usually left out of garlands quite deliberately; but not, apparently, in Oxford, where they are used, seemingly without ill effects, by any May-keeping children who may feel so disposed.

At Charlton-on-Otmoor, there is in the church a large wooden cross, covered with clipped yew and box, which stands above the rood screen. This is known as The Garland. On May Day (and also on 19 September, the village feast), it is taken down and dressed anew with fresh greenery and flowers. On May Day also, the children carry small flower-decorated crosses about the village, and bring them to a special service in the church.

An interesting history lies behind these customs. Before the Reformation, two statues stood upon the rood screen, one of Our Lady and the other of St John. That of Our Lady used to be carried across the moor with ceremony on May Day, to the Benedictine Priory at Studley. Both these statues disappeared during the turmoils of the English Reformation, but the villagers replaced them by two green hooped garlands. One was larger than the other, and according to some nineteenth-century illustrations, both vaguely resembled a roughly made human figure. For so long as they remained in existence, they used to be redressed on May Day, and carried about the village and the fields, with music and Morris dancing. The larger of the two, like Our Lady's image of old, was taken in procession over the moor to the private house which had succeeded to the pre-Reformation Priory at Studley. Meanwhile, the smaller garland was carried about in Charlton by the women and children. The rest of the day was spent in dancing and merriment, and in due course, the hoop figures – latterly only one, since the other seems to have disappeared at some time before 1840 – were restored to their places above the rood screen. These festival customs came to an end in 1857, but the ceremonial redressing first of the hoop garland and then of the wooden cross that took its place, went on without a break, and continues still today.

Another famous garland ceremony is that which takes place at Abbotsbury, in Dorset, on Garland Day, which is 13 May (Old May Day). This is now simply a village custom, of a type that might be found elsewhere, but originally it had a maritime association. Abbotsbury, formerly, had a fishing fleet of a dozen

boats or more, all of them local-owned and manned by local
crews. The fishing season began on 13 May, and on that day
every boat had its own flower garland, which was taken at noon
to the parish church to be blessed at a special service. Afterwards
there was dancing and games on the green below the castle, and
on the beach. Then, towards evening, the boats put out to sea,
each with a garland in the bow and, at a certain distance from the
shore, all the garlands were thrown overboard, while a song was
sung, or a prayer was said. No one now seems to remember
what the song was, only that it was sung while the garlands sank, or floated away. This ceremony, which was never
omitted, was believed to be essential for the luck of the fishing
season.

Now there are no more fishing boats at Abbotsbury, but the
children still have traditional flower garlands, mounted upon
short poles, which they carry about the village, visiting each house
in turn to bring luck to the inmates, and receiving small gifts
of money in return. When the visiting is over, the money is shared
out among the children. But the garlands, which were once meant
to bring good fortune to the boats, never now come to the sea.
At the day's end, they are laid at the foot of the War Memorial.

The local people claim that their garland custom runs back for
a thousand years, or more, and undoubtedly it is of great age.
In 1954, an attempt to suppress it was made by an over-zealous
policeman, a newcomer to the district, who had apparently not yet
had time to get to know his people, and obviously knew nothing
at all about folk customs. He stopped the children as they went on
their garland-bearing rounds, confiscated the money they had
so far collected, and told them they were breaking the law by
begging. This action infuriated the villagers to such an extent
that they immediately complained to the Chief Constable of
Dorset, and made their feelings even plainer by organizing, on the
following day, a procession of protest against the attempted
destruction of their age-old tradition. As a result, the custom was
saved, and Garland Day was officially acknowledged as one of
Abbotsbury's established anniversaries. There is, however, little
doubt that had the parishioners been less prompt and less firm
in its defence, the story might well have ended differently.

The Maypole has always been an essential part of the May
celebrations because it represents the Summer that is just beginning, and the great upsurging force of fertility and growth that is

felt at full strength at this time. For that reason, the Puritans hated it wholeheartedly, as indeed, they hated everything connected with May Day. Stubbes called it a 'stinking Idol', and he meant what he said; and the Ordinance of 1644 which forbade (along with much else) its erection or maintenance anywhere in England and Wales, referred to it as 'a heathenish vanity generally abused to superstition and wickedness'. Many hundreds of poles came down all over the country as a result of that Ordinance, some men hastening to bring them down from genuine religious feeling, and some through fear of the fines imposed upon those who left them standing. But many others bitterly resented the loss of their traditional poles, and resisted it as long as they could. When Adam Martindale was minister at Rostherne in Cheshire, not all his fiery eloquence could persuade his stubborn parishioners to destroy their Maypole. There it stood, and there it seemed likely to remain, until Mrs Martindale took the law into her own hands. Without a word to her husband, she quietly went out one night with a handsaw and, with the help of three stalwart young women, cut down the offending pole, leaving only a short stump, which she said would serve as a dial post. Here and there, in some remote place, a Maypole might be left standing on its customary site, perhaps to remain unmolested through all the years of the Commonwealth, though no one dared to hold the traditional revels round it. After the Restoration, however, they all came back into favour, and have remained a distinctive feature of the May celebrations from then on down to our own times.

Many of the Maypoles we see today, especially those used in school May Day ceremonies, are of that short, beribboned type, which was introduced into this country from southern Europe in 1888. Round this, the children danced a plaited-ribbon dance, with coloured ribbons streaming from the top of the pole, which is very pretty when properly done, but quite untraditional. The real English Maypole is the tall, straight shaft, sometimes with brightly coloured rings or spirals painted on it, which is usually (though not always) a permanent erection, standing on a traditional site throughout the year, and decorated with wreaths and ribbons and greenery when May Day comes round once more. Although the site is often ancient, the pole itself is never very old, for after about 15 years of life, it begins to rot at the foot, and has to be renewed. At Temple Sowerby in Westmorland the duty of renewing the Maypole on the green falls upon the Lord of the Manor.

The normal height of such poles is 60 to 80ft. The famous Maypole in the Strand, which was set up in 1661, on the first May Day after Charles II's return, was 134ft high, but that was exceptional, and so was the length of its life, for it stood for about 50 years, until Sir Isaac Newton removed it in 1717, to be used in supporting a reflecting telescope. The church of St Andrew Undershaft in Leadenhall Street was so named because the great Maypole that annually stood before the south door was taller than the church itself. It was one of those poles which were erected every year, as it was needed, taken down when the festivities were over, and then set up again on the following May Day. It hung for many years upon hooks under the eaves of the houses on one side of Shaft Alley, but in 1552 it was destroyed, as the result of a sermon preached by a curate of St Katharine's Church. This man, calling it, like Stubbes, an idol, induced the residents of the Alley to pull it down, and cut it into pieces, each man taking as much wood as lay along the eaves of his own house, for firewood.

The permanent shaft at Welford-on-Avon, splendid with its scarlet spirals, stands 70ft high, that on Pagan Hill at Stroud 80ft. Other very tall Maypoles exist at Wellow, Slingsby, Preston Brockenhurst, Upper Poppleton, and elsewhere. At Barwick-in-Elmet, in Yorkshire, an 80ft pole is taken down every three years, on Easter Monday, to be repainted, repaired, and when it becomes necessary, renewed. At the same time, the four garlands, made of rosettes, ribbons and flowers, are restored. All these arrangements are under the direction of three elected Pole Men. On Whit Tuesday, the Maypole is set up again, all the customary May ceremonies are held instead of on 1 May, and the pole is then left in position until the time to restore and redecorate it comes round once more.

The name ' Maypole ' is (or was, so long as there were horses on the farm), also given in Herefordshire to the tall birch sapling, dressed with red and white streamers, which, until very recently, used to be brought in on May morning, and set up against the stable door. There it was left all through the year, to protect the horses from being ' hag-ridden ' by night, and generally to nullify the effects of witchcraft. In Shrewsbury, the children have their own special Maypole ceremony, in which the ' Maypole ' is a pram wheel, decorated with coloured paper, and set on top of a pole in such a manner that it revolves. The pole is usually about 3 or 5ft high. A band of children goes from house to house, led by a crowned Queen who sits on a wooden stool, holding up the Maypole, while the others dance and sing, and a collection is taken from the householders and passers-by.

May Queens nowadays are almost always children, but this is a custom which appears to owe its existence mainly to Ruskin who, along with the short Maypole and the plaited-ribbon dance, introduced the idea of a child-Queen and a Coronation ceremony at Whitelands College in 1888. Earlier, the May Queen was not a child, but a young woman chosen for her popularity and beauty, and usually accompanied by a May King. In some districts there was no King or Queen, but a Lord and Lady, who jointly represented the Summer, and presided over all the May celebrations. They were not crowned, and of the two, the Lord was the more important. He was often responsible for choosing the Lady. Where this custom still exists, as it does in some Oxfordshire villages, the Lord flourishes as of old, but the May King seems to have disappeared almost everywhere, and in most places is not even remembered. The Queen is left to reign alone, and is crowned with great ceremony by her predecessor, or by some local notable.

At Knutsford, on their famous Royal May Day, they have no May King, though they have almost everything else. This festival is not necessarily held on 1 May, but can be on any convenient day during the month. Its history is rather uncertain. In 1864, it was described as a ' revival ', but in his *Cheshire* (1932), T. A. Coward suggests that originally the celebrations belonged, not to Knutsford, but to Rostherne, which was the ancient Church Town of the parish in which Knutsford was included. The latter did not become a separate parish until 1744. The May festival acquired the right to call itself Royal in 1887, after it had been visited by the Prince and Princess of Wales (later Edward VII and Queen Alexandra). In its modern form, the celebration is very elaborate, with a long procession winding through the streets of the town on to Knutsford Heath, where there is a Maypole, and where the Queen is crowned. The town's famous sedan chair appears in the procession, and so do the Queen's maids-of-honour, sword-bearer, and attendants, the Morris dancers, Robin Hood and Maid Marian, and Jack-in-the-Green. On this day, the streets are sanded, as they still are for weddings and special occasions also. Mottoes and other designs are traced on the pavements (or in the case of a wedding, outside the doors of bride, groom, and guests), with white sand trickled through a funnel on to a groundwork of brown sand. This custom seems to be peculiar to Knutsford, and is sometimes explained locally by a very improbable tale concerning King Canute crossing the river Lily.

Jack-in-the-Green, who appears on Royal May Day, is not very often seen now, but he is nevertheless an important character of the Spring Festival, the English equivalent of the continental Green George. He wears a heavy wicker cage completely covered with greenery, so that only his eyes and his feet are visible, and in that green disguise he represents one aspect of the summer, as the May King and Queen represent another. In the eighteenth century, he became rather oddly involved with the young chimney-sweeps of London and other big towns and became the central figure of the sweeps' procession. This custom died out gradually after 1840, when it ceased to be legal to employ young boys as chimney-sweeps, but at least as late as the turn of the century, Jack-in-the-Green continued to appear in his own ancient character in the summer rituals of many places.

The May festival at Padstow begins at midnight on May Eve, with the Mayers going about in the darkness, singing the ' Night Song ' and visiting various houses to serenade and greet those within by name. In the morning, the Hobby Horse appears from the Golden Lion Inn, which is, and has been for a long time, his headquarters. He is the centre of all the day's festivities, locally known as Old Oss, or Obby Oss, a very strange creature indeed, which resembles neither horse nor human, but seems to have come direct from some other and more terrifying world than this. His body is completely hidden by a large, tarpaulin-covered hoop, about 6ft in diameter, his face by a savage-looking mask, above which rises a high, conical hat. With him go a variety of attendants, but the chief of these is his Teaser, who carries a padded club, and changes his festival attire from year to year.

Off they go through the streets, where the ' Night Song ' is still being sung continuously. The Oss chases the women, and from time to time captures one of them under his great tarpaulin skirt. This is supposed to bring her good luck, in the form of a husband within 12 months if she is unmarried, or a baby in the same period, if she is already wed. Once she came out from under the tarpaulin with her face or her dress marked with black, from the blacklead or tar then smeared on the underside of the cloth, but this part of the custom has vanished now. Similarly, a rain-making rite that was once part of the ceremonies has gone. The Oss and all his followers used to go to Treator Pool, where the Oss drank the water, and all the people were sprinkled with it. This was given up about 1930, for the curious reason that the Pool was considered too far from the town for the people to walk to it.

From time to time, the Hobby-Horse died. The lively 'Night Song', with its gay tune and its happy reiterated assertion that 'Summer is i-comen in today', changes to the slow and dirge-like 'Day Song', with its strange, and by now incomprehensible words,

> O, where is St George? O, where is he, O?
> He's out in his long-boat, all on the salt sea, O.
> Up flies the kite, down falls the lark, O.
> Aunt Ursula Birdwood, she had an old ewe,
> But it died in her own Park, O.

Down sinks the Oss and crouches on the ground, as though he were dying, while his Teaser pats him consolingly with his club. Suddenly, he comes to life again, leaps high up in the air, and falls to dancing and capering once more, while the 'Night Song' bursts out again, and everybody sings:

> Unite, unite, and let us all unite,
> For Summer is i-comen in today,
> And whither we are going, we will all unite,
> In this merry morning of May.

By late afternoon, Old Oss and his company have reached the great Maypole in the market place, and there, for the first time that day, he meets Padstow's second Hobby-Horse, variously known as the Temperance, or Blue Ribbon, or Peace Horse. This creature closely resembles the traditional beast, and has his own Teaser and followers. He and his attendant Mayers came into existence at the end of World War I. The two groups do not collide in the May Day festivities, but follow their own time-tables, and take their own course round the town, to meet finally, and amicably, by the Maypole in the square.

There is another May Day Hobby-Horse at Minehead in Somerset, as old as Padstow's Old Oss, and as impressive, but altogether different in appearance. This is the Sailors' Horse, who lives on the Quayside, and comes out first on May Eve, which is known as Warning Night, and then again on May Day itself. He wears a horse-cloth, adorned with painted rings, and stretched over a flat pasteboard frame. On the top of this frame is a bright jumble of short coloured streamers, looking rather like a thick rag mat. There is a long rope tail, and once there was a horse's head with snapping jaws, but that has disappeared now. The horse-man wears a high, pointed cap, and his human face is hidden by a mask of very ferocious aspect.

At six o'clock on May morning, the Horse and his companions go out to a cross-road not far from the town, and there he bows to the rising sun. Once, a May Queen was chosen then, and was allowed to ride on the Horse's back. Nowadays, this part of the ceremony has been forgotten, and only a few people accompany the Horse to the cross-roads in the early morning. He used to be attended on his rounds by two men, wearing masks and tall head-dresses, and sometimes armed with a whip, or a pair of tongs. There were the Gullivers, who acted as collectors, and were not above frightening people when they thought it necessary. Anyone who was grudging with his gifts, or ill-mannered, or otherwise tiresome, was liable to be ' booted ', that is, tied up with the Horse's long rope tail, and beaten with a boot that was carried for the purpose. The Gullivers had other methods of extracting largesse, and seem to have been rather alarming characters; nevertheless, they, like the Horse, were luck-bringers, and house doors along the route were left open for all three to enter and pass right through the house. They are gone, now, but the Hobby-Horse still makes his rounds on May Day, first paying a ceremonial visit to Dunster Castle, where the Luttrell family receives him with honour, and then spending the rest of the day parading through Dunster and Minehead, and dancing a few steps outside the various houses. It may be added that, contrary to general opinion, the Minehead Hobby-Horse is not, and never was, intended to represent a ship.

Furry Day is the great May festival of Helston, in Cornwall, when every house and building is bright with sycamore and beech, flowers and greenery of all kinds, and the ancient Furry Dance is danced in the streets. The date is 8 May, which is also the

Feast of the Apparition of St Michael, the patron saint of the town. Very early in the morning, some of the young people go out into the woods to gather green branches, and then, returning home again, they parade through the streets, accompanied by young men dressed as St Michael and St George, Robin Hood, Little John, and Friar Tuck. At various fixed points along the way, they stop to sing ' Hal-an-Tow ', the ancient song which proclaims very clearly what they are about :

> With Hal-an-Tow! Jolly Rumble, O!
> For we are up as soon as any day, O,
> And for to fetch the Summer home,
> The Summer and the May, O.
> For Summer is a-come, O,
> And winter is a-gone, O.

Meanwhile, precisely at seven o'clock, other young people perform the first dance of the day, which used to be called the Maidservants' Dance. At ten o'clock the Children's Dance begins, with children from all the schools, dressed in white and wearing lilies-of-the-valley, the special flower of the day, as their predecessors in the Early Morning dance did also. At noon, the chief, or Invitation Dance begins, led by the Mayor and made up of men and women dancing in couples, the women in their best summer dresses, and the men in morning coats and top hats. Through the narrow streets they go, some of them quite steep in this hilly town, dancing all the way, and now and then swerving from the main route to enter a house or a shop, and bring the Luck of Summer to those within. They bow, or curtsey to whoever they meet inside and, if it is possible, they dance right through the house, and out again at the back. At half-past one, the dance ends, and the somewhat breathless dancers are entertained to luncheon at the Guildhall.

The last dance of the day is at five o'clock, and is led by the Early Morning dancers. But in the last stage of this one, the spectators are allowed to take part, and as nearly everybody does, it seems at the day's close as though the whole town was dancing together. To be asked to lead any of the day's dances is a very great honour, and there is a strict rule that the leading couples of each dance must always be Helston-born. Local legends say the dancing began long ago, when St Michael and the Devil fought for possession of the town and St Michael won. The people danced in the streets then for joy and relief, and tradition says they have done so ever since on the anniversary, without a break, except in times of war or plague. Actually, there can be no doubt that the Furry Dance is pre-Christian in origin, and formed part of the communal spring festival, intended, as the ' Hal-an-Tow ' says, ' for to fetch the Summer home '. Similar dances survived at one time at the Lizard on 1 May, and at Penryn on 3 May, but of these, no trace now remains.

The last festival of the month of May is Oak Apple Day, which falls on 29 May. This is the anniversary of that happy day in 1660 when Charles II ' came into his own again ', riding into London on his 30th birthday through dense crowds wild with joy. He had been an exile for nine years while his people languished under Cromwellian dictatorship; and now he was returning home again, bringing back with him, not only the traditional rule of kings natural to the country, but also freedom, and laughter, and the old kindly ways of everyday life. 'From this day,' wrote the Rector of Maids Moreton in his church register, ' ancient orders began to be observed, *Laus Deo.*'

The day is variously known by several names – Royal Oak Day, Oak Apple Day, Shick Shack Day, Oak and Nettle Day in some districts, and Oaken Bough Day, or Oak Ball Day elsewhere. Of all Charles's many adventures during his long absence, nothing impressed his people so much as his concealment in the oak after the Battle of Worcester. In the celebrations of his Restoration, the oak branch and the oak apple figure everywhere. For nearly three centuries, oak leaves, were customarily worn then, and oak apples, if they could be had. Those who did not wear these loyal emblems were liable to be pinched, or kicked, or more usually, beaten with nettles. Houses also were decorated with oak boughs, or leaves, and so were shop windows in many districts, and the towers of churches. Horses had their harness adorned with oak sprigs and oak apples; and until the turn of the century, or a little later, it was not at all surprising to see a train steaming into the station with its engine smothered in greenery.

Oak Apple Day was a very well-loved festival from the beginning, and in its heyday, it tended to absorb some of the existing festal customs, especially those of May Day. In some parts of the Midlands, the Maypole ceremonies were almost as usual on the 29th day of the month as they were on the first. In her *Folk-Lore of Herefordshire* (1912) Mrs Leather relates that an informant told her: ' The twenty-ninth was our real May Day in Bromyard. You'd see Maypoles all the way down Sheep Street, decorated with oak boughs and flowers, and people dancing round them, all wearing oak leaves.' At Shillingstone, in Dorset, the Maypole standing on the green is decorated with wreaths on 9 June, though no one now dances round it. This rather curious date is a fruit of the calendar change in 1752. Originally, there was dancing and a kind of unofficial fair here on May Day, which, in the course of time, was shifted to Oak Apple Day, as a manifestation of loyalty. Then, when the calendar was altered, the festival was advanced a further 11 days (as was the case with many old customs then), and now falls on, or about 9 June. The dancing and the fair have vanished now, but the Maypole remains, and the wreaths hung on it in June are allowed to hang there until they wither.

At Castleton in Derbyshire the Garland King custom seems almost certainly to have been transferred at some time from 1 May to Oak Apple Day. A procession goes round the village, led by the Garland King, a man on horseback, who wears a great wooden cage, covered with flowers and greenery, over his head and shoulders. This is the Garland, on the top of which is a posy of specially fine flowers, known as the Queen. Behind the King rides another ' Queen ', this time a human being, veiled and riding side-saddle, who, until 1956, was always a man dressed in women's clothes. In that year, however, there was a change, and the traditional Man–Woman's place was taken by a girl, and has been ever since.

As the procession makes its way round the village, it stops at certain fixed points to allow the dancers to perform. Once, these were the bell-ringers, who danced with oak sprays in their hands, and moreover, were responsible for the organization of all the ceremonies; but now it is schoolgirls, dressed in white, who dance, and an elected Garland committee runs the festivities.

At the end of the procession, the King rides into the churchyard, and the great Garland is lifted from his head. The Queen-posy is taken from it, and then it is hauled up to the top of the tower, and fixed to one of the pinnacles. Formerly, it was left there until next Garland Day came round, or until high winds and bad weather destroyed it, but now it is taken down after a short while, and stowed away with the rest of the festival properties. The Queen-posy used to be presented to some admired local personage as the greatest honour the bell-ringers had to bestow; now, for much the same reason, it is laid by the King at the foot of the war memorial.

Of the straightforward memorial customs connected with Royal Oak Day, the best known is Founder's Day, at the Royal Hospital, Chelsea. This hostel for soldiers incapacitated by old age or disability was founded by Charles II in 1682, and once a year, on or near 29 May, his birthday is remembered with affection and ceremony. His statue in the main court is covered with oak boughs. All the pensioners wear oak sprigs, and so does the special visitor – usually a member of the Royal Family, or perhaps a famous general – who comes to watch the ceremonial march past of the scarlet-clad veterans. At a much older soldiers' hospital, the Leycester Hospital in Warwick, all the rooms and galleries are hung with oak on 29 May, and a special issue of food and drink is made to the men. At Worcester, that loyal city, they remember both the battle in 1651, and the triumph nine years later, with a civic ceremony, and the hanging of the Guild Hall gates with oak boughs. And in Northampton, they remember not only the King's return, but also a thousand tons of timber from Whittlebury Forest which he gave them (together with a remission of hearth tax for seven years) in 1675, after much of the town had been destroyed by a disastrous fire. Here there is a procession from the town hall to All Saints' Church led by the Mayor and corporation all carrying oak apples and gilded leaves, and including a company of schoolchildren bearing the same loyal signs. The statue of Charles outside the church is also decorated with oak branches for the occasion.

# 6 High Summer

BETWEEN MAY DAY and the first of August comes that golden season of high summer which runs through May and June, and up to the crown of the year at midsummer, and then passes onwards through July and into the first beginnings of autumn at Lammas-tide. A variety of long-established festivals, ecclesiastical and secular, are remembered during this time. Whitsun is one of them, that great feast of the Church which falls 50 days after Easter, but because it is dependent upon Easter, varies in its own date, and may be as early as the middle of May, or as late as 13 June. Ascension Day is another, and so are the Rogation Days which immediately precede it, when in many parishes still, the bounds are beaten, and the fields or harbours blessed.

Rogationtide consists of the fifth Sunday after Easter, and the Monday, Tuesday, and Wednesday that follow it, leading up to Ascension. The name Rogation derives from *rogere,* meaning to ask or beseech, and what is asked or besought at this time is God's blessing on the crops, or on the fisheries of the sea. From

F

as far back as the fifth century AD, Christian processions have gone about the fields of Western Europe, and litanies have been sung as they went for this purpose. Mamertus, Bishop of Vienne, ordered this to be done on Ascension Day, or on the three preceding days, in AD 470, during a period of plague and earthquake, and from then onwards, the custom spread slowly to other parts of the Christian world. It reached England in the eighth century. In some northern districts still, the old name of Gang Week, or Ganging Days, is occasionally used for Rogation-tide and Ascension, from the Anglo-Saxon *gangen*, to go, because at this time the people *gang*, or go about the parish, to bless the fields and beat the bounds.

'Processioning' at Rogation-tide was frowned upon in the early years of the Reformation, but in the reign of Queen Elizabeth, the clergy were, if not actually instructed, at least permitted to perambulate their parishes, as of old. Perhaps one of the reasons for this restoration of former custom, apart from real religious feeling, was the widely acknowledged usefulness of the bound-beating which usually formed part of the ceremonies. It was essential that every man who lived in a parish, rural or urban, should know quite clearly the limits of that parish; and when maps were few and most people illiterate, the easiest way to ensure that everyone concerned did know was for all to follow the line and visit each landmark in person at least once a year. Children and young lads, especially, had the nature and situation of each mark impressed upon their memories by more than merely visual contact. They were bumped upon boundary stones, dragged through hedges and ditches, thrown into streams and ponds, forced to climb over the roofs of buildings that straddled the line, and sometimes beaten with rods at particular points by their elders. At the end of it all, they were rewarded with gifts of money, or cakes, or willow wands. It was then believed by everyone that they would never forget this rough-and-tumble experience, and that years afterwards, in any case of dispute, they would be able to speak with authority of the boundary line along which they had once endured so much discomfort and pain. Probably, in every parish, there were always a number of old or middle-aged men who could testify in this way from their own childhood experience, but in every generation, a new band of fresh young witnesses were enrolled in the same manner.

Now the need for this form of 'memory-training' exists no

longer, but the bounds are still beaten in a variety of parishes. Mostly it is the boundary marks themselves which are beaten today, with white willow wands that the boys carry for the purpose. In the Tower of London, where the bounds are beaten on Ascension Day, once in every three years, a procession of Yeoman Warders in scarlet and gold, commanded by the Resident Governor in full dress, the Chaplain, the choirboys in red cassocks and carrying willow wands, and the Tower residents, perambulate the Tower limits, and stop at each of the 39 Crown Boundary Marks. Beside each one, the Chaplain says in a loud voice, ' Cursed be he who removeth his neighbour's land mark ', and the Chief Warder calls, ' Whack it, boys, whack it!', and the boys bring down their wands upon the mark with the greatest enthusiasm. The London parish of St Clement Danes has 25 surviving marks, each bearing the anchor of St Clement upon it. One of these marks is now below ground level, and in order to reach it, a choirboy has to be held by the heels and lowered towards it so that he may strike it. Part of the boundary of this parish runs down the middle of the river Thames, and the procession therefore has to take to boats for that part of their journey.

At Lichfield, elm boughs are carried on Ascension Day, and clergymen and choristers halt at eight places along the route where wells once existed. At each one, the Gospel is read, and part of a psalm is sung. Afterwards, all return to the cathedral, a blessing is given by the font, and the elm boughs are left round it. This religious ceremony has nothing to do with that other perambulation of the city which is known as the Sheriff's Ride, and takes place on 8 September. The latter is a purely secular event. In Oxford, the boundary lines of two parishes run through college quads, one through All Souls and the other through Lincoln. Here, after the marks have been duly beaten, the Fellows throw hot pennies to be scrambled for by the boys. Along the coasts, Rogation ceremonies in some parishes have more to do with the sea than with the fields. It is the nets, and the boats and those who sail in them, and sometimes the sea itself, which are blessed. At Brixham, on Rogation Sunday, there is an open-air service by the waterside, as there is at Hastings and one or two places along the Kentish coast on other days of the same week, and also at Mudeford, in Hampshire. At Cullercoats in Northumberland, clergy and choir sail out into the harbour to bless the boats, and so they do at North Shields where, after the blessing, they sail some way up the river Tyne, which here forms part of the boundary between North and South Shields.

A curious custom is kept up on Ascension Eve, on the river shore at Boyes Staith, Whitby. The Horngarth, or Penny Hedge, is annually planted there, below high-water mark, the ' hedge ' consisting of a stout fence of stakes and interlaced oisers, which has to be strong enough to withstand three consecutive tides. This is really a tenure custom, connected with certain lands held once from the Abbey of Whitby by the service of erecting this fence in the water. How old it is is uncertain; it is said by some to run back to Anglo-Saxon times, and it is quite possible that it does. Legend, however, puts its origin in the twelfth century. According to a local tale, three young men, whose names are still remembered, went out hunting on 16 October 1159 in the abbot's woods on Eskdale-side. There they started a boar, which eventually ran for shelter into the chapel of a hermit who lived in these woods. He shut the chapel door in their faces, with the boar safe inside, and this so enraged the hunters that they beat the unhappy man within an inch of death. He did die shortly afterwards, but not before he had forgiven them, and had persuaded the Abbot of Whitby to accept a penance of his (the hermit's) own choosing instead of the penalties for murder and sacrilege which were the hunters' due.

They and their descendants were henceforth to hold their lands from the Abbey by the annual building of the Horngarth. They were to go at sunrise on Ascension Eve to Stray Head Wood, and in the presence of the abbot's bailiff, cut a number of stakes and osiers with a knife ' valued at one penny '. These stakes they were to carry through the town and down to the river, and there they had to construct their fence. At intervals, while the work was being done, and at its end, the abbot's bailiff was to blow his horn, and cry ' Owte upon ye! Owte upon ye!' in memory of their crime.

Upon the due performance of this service depended the tenancy of the abbey lands held by the families of the three men concerned. Now the abbey is in ruins, the monks dispersed and dead long since, and the lands passed into other hands. But the old service is still rendered for part of the original territories to the lord of the manor of Whitby who has taken the place of the abbot in this, and in some other matters. The tenant now is excused the cutting of the wood with a knife 'valued at one penny', and its public carriage through the town; but he has to be at the water's edge at nine o'clock in the morning on Ascension Eve, and there build his strong hedge, fit to resist the onslaughts of three tides. This is not easy work and there is little wonder that he is nearly always surrounded by an admiring crowd while he does it. The manor bailiff is present also, and when the hedge is finished, he blows an ancient horn, and cries 'Out upon ye! Out upon ye!' with as much enthusiasm as ever his predecessor, the abbot's bailiff, did in the Middle Ages.

Whit Sunday is one of the great feasts of the Church, and the one or two days that follow it have always been occasions for festivals and jollifications of all sorts. Or at least, they were until the government abolished the old Whit Monday Bank Holiday, and replaced it with another falling on the last Monday in May, and bearing the somewhat meaningless name of the Spring Holiday. In 1871, when the Bank Holidays Act was passed, all the new official holidays were named after the Church festivals with which these anniversaries had always been connected, with the exception of one, on the first Monday in August, which did not replace anything in particular. Now there are two such holidays with secular names and no ancient connections, and a fine confusion between the old Whit Monday and its customs and the new spring date. It is usually necessary today to enquire, before attending any given Whitsun feast, whether it is still held on the traditional day, or whether, for the sake of convenience, it has been transferred to the last Monday in May.

The Whitsun Ales, which used to be the main feature of the festivities in countless parishes, have vanished now, primarily because the money they provided for the parish needs is now obtained in other ways. In their heyday, they were pleasant and happy occasions when, as Aubrey tells us in his account of Wiltshire, ' the housekeepers met, and were merry, and gave their charity ', and the young people danced and played games. There was usually an elected Lord and Lady of the Ale, or a Whitsun King and Queen, who presided over the whole affair, Morris dancers and often a Summer Bower made of green branches, sometimes even a Maypole, as there was at Woodstock, where the Whitsun Ale lasted from Ascension Eve until the end of Whit Week. The last Maypole to be erected perished one night in 1843, having been left standing after the festivities were finally ended. It was then sold, but before the buyer could take it away, some members of the Yeomanry, then stationed in the town, pulled it down out of sheer lightness of heart, and destroyed it.

Whitsun is the heyday of the Morris dancers' season, though they often appear on May Day, and some times earlier, and may be met on various occasions afterwards during almost the whole of the summer. At Bampton, in Oxfordshire, they go about the town on Whit Monday, which is also the day of the old Club Feast, dancing in the streets and in a variety of private gardens, where they are always very welcome. With them goes a sword-bearer, carrying a cake impaled on the end of his sword. Small slices of this cake are sold to the spectators, to bring them fertility and good luck. The team here is said to be the oldest in England, having, it is claimed, a continuous and unbroken history of 500 years' span. Not far off, at Abingdon, there is another well-known Morris side which possesses a fine ox head with springing horns as a sign, carried on the top of a pole. Once a year, on or about 19 June, the residents of Ock Street elect a mayor for the side. They cast their votes by inserting ballot slips into a wooden box that stands on a table in the open street. When he has been duly elected, the Morris Mayor is ' danced in ', first in Ock Street, and then in other parts of the town. However, this is not really a Whitsuntide ceremony, because the date of the election is fixed by the Feast of St Edmund of Abingdon, who was born in the town in 1180, and eventually became Archbishop of Canterbury.

On Whit Sunday still, there is a distribution of bread and cheese at St Briavels, in Gloucestershire. As soon as the evening service is over, baskets of bread and cheese are carried to a narrow lane near the church, and from the top of a high wall running along it, the food is thrown to the waiting people, who scramble for it. Once, the whole ceremony took place inside the church, the bread and cheese being tossed from the galleries among the departing congregation. Later, this was considered unseemly, and instead, the baskets were emptied from the top of the tower and the contents scrambled for in the churchyard. This, however, caused damage to some of the graves, and eventually the distribution was transferred to the lane where it is made now. The custom, which is very old, is said to be strictly necessary in order to maintain the commoners' rights of grazing, and of cutting timber in Hudnall's Wood.

Cheese-rolling down the precipitous face of Cooper's Hill,

near Brockworth, also in Gloucestershire, is another Whitsuntide custom of considerable antiquity. It now takes place on the Spring Holiday, but formerly it was held on Whit Monday. Near the top of the hill, there is a space on which stands a tall Maypole, which is decorated with flowers for this occasion, but is too steeply placed for dancing round it. Here the young people of the neighbourhood gather in the early evening, with the Master of Ceremonies in his white coat and beribboned hat, and another man who has been asked to act as Starter of the races for that year. At the beginning of the race (of which there are usually several during the evening), the Starter, at the behest of the Master, sets the cheese running and bouncing down the hillside, and immediately afterwards, all the young racers stream after it. As the slope is very severe and the ground very rough, most of them fall before long, and many roll, rather than run, a fair way before the end is reached. But nobody minds, and the cheese itself is protected on its wild flight downwards by the very skilled and careful wrapping. It is, of course, the first prize in the contest, and there are also money prizes for the runners-up. Like the St Briavels bread-and-cheese distribution, the rolling is said to be a necessary ritual for the maintenance of certain grazing rights in the parish.

The Ram Roasting Fair at Kingsteignton, in Devon, was once a two-day celebration, extending over Whit Monday and Tuesday, but towards the end of last century, it became a one-day affair, first on the Tuesday, and later, on the Monday. At one time, a living ram lamb used to be drawn about the streets in a decorated cart on the first day, honoured and made much of, and then, on the Tuesday, killed and roasted on a great open-air fire. Now the living animal is no longer carried about, but a garlanded carcase is paraded through the town before it is roasted. While it is cooking, sports, games, and dancing take place in the field. By tradition, everyone present ought to have a slice of the sacrificial meat when it is ready, and so they did once, but now the great crowds who come to the fair every year make this impossible. Instead, numbered programmes are issued, certain numbers conferring the right to a share of the meat upon those who possess them.

The origin of this curious custom does not seem to be certainly known. Legend, however, connects it directly with the Fairwater, a stream which is said never to run dry, even in times of drought, and was, until piped water was brought to the village in 1895, a main source of the local water supply. But once, apparently, it did run dry, long ago, in pre-Christian times. The local people sacrificed a ram lamb in the dry bed of the stream, and immediately, the water began to run again. Thereafter a lamb was regularly offered every year, originally, no doubt, to ensure that the Fairwater never ran dry again, and later, perhaps, in thanksgiving that it has not, so far, done so.

A somewhat similar but much more elaborate ceremony flourished at Kirtlington, in Oxfordshire, until 1858. This was the Lamb Ale, which began on Trinity Monday, and lasted for eight or nine days afterwards. There was a Lord, chosen by the young men of the village, and a Lady, chosen by the Lord and his friends. These two presided over the festivities and the processions, each one carrying a Mace as a badge of office. These Maces were flat square boards set on a short staff, with intersecting half hoops attached to the corners, like a garland, the whole Mace being covered with pink and blue silk and adorned with rosettes and long ribbon streamers. There was also a Fool, in motley, Morris dancers and musicians, two men carrying 'Forest Feathers', which were decorated wooden clubs, and above all, the Lamb. This little creature was the centre of the whole celebration, and was carried in procession on the Monday, Tuesday, and Wednesday. Then he – or perhaps, since he had to be the best in the parish, a less valuable substitute – was killed, and made into pies, which were cut up and distributed to the people as luck-bringers. Only one, the Head Pie, which contained the head with some wool still on it, had to be sold undivided. The rest of the eight or nine days was spent in drinking in the Bowery, a hut specially made of green boughs, where ale was sold without a licence, in dancing and merriment, and visits by the Morris dancers to all the villages within reach, to dance there and collect money for the expenses of the Lamb Ale.

There is no explanatory legend to account for this custom, but clearly, like the Kingsteignton Ram Roasting, it represented the sacrifice of a living animal for the good of the whole community, and had its beginnings far back in time. It ended in 1858, but its memory is still kept alive in its old home by the fact that Trinity Monday, the old Village Feast-day, is always known as the Lamb Ale, and that on this day, the main dish at the traditional dinner is always roast lamb.

Little is left now of the Midsummer Festival, far less in England than is the case in Sweden, or the Pyrenees, or in Hungary. For many people here it is simply Quarter Day, when bills and rents have to be paid. Nevertheless, some of the ancient glamour of Midsummer, the Crown of Summer, the Turn of the Year, still clings about it. Not that it really is the Turn of the Year, for that comes a few days earlier, at the summer solstice, on which day, very probably, the great magical fires of renewal and protection were lit in remote pre-Christian times. But 24 June is, and has been since the fifth century AD, the Feast of the Nativity of St John the Baptist, that saint whose name has always been associated in folk tradition with bonfires and the sun's slow decline into winter. He it was who said, speaking of Christ and of himself, ' He must increase, and I must decrease ' (John, 3 : 30). and of whose feast-day (then new), St Augustine, about AD 430, said the Midsummer date was appropriate because after it the days began to shorten, whereas after the Birthday of Our Lord on Christmas Day, they began steadily to lengthen. From the beginning, the new feast borrowed the pagan fires that were the main features of the old heathen festival. Bonfires blazed upon hill-tops all over Europe, burning tar barrels were pushed about the streets, and flaming wheels rolled down steep slopes, only now all this was said to be done in honour of the Christian saint, instead of being part of a solar ritual intended to strengthen the sun at the beginning of its long road downwards to the winter solstice.

Fire and magic were the principal elements of the Midsummer Festival, as it used to be celebrated. John Stow, in his *Survey*, tells us how fires were lit in the streets of Elizabethan London after sunset, ' every man bestowing wood and labour towards them ', and how ' on the Vigil of St John the Baptist . . . every man's door being shadowed with green birch, long fennel, St John's wort, orpin, white lilies, and such like, garnished upon with garlands of beautiful flowers, had also lamps of glass, with oil burning in them all the night; some hung out branches of iron curiously wrought containing hundreds of lamps alight at once, which made a goodly show.' All the plants that he mentioned here were believed to have magical properties, and were used at this season in charms and divinations, especially St John's wort, which was itself a sun symbol on account of its gold flower, and had protective and fertility-inducing powers.

There was also the rare and dangerous fern seed, which he does not mention, but which could only be gathered at midnight on Midsummer Eve. Whoever had the courage to collect it then would henceforth be able to find hidden treasure, summon any living creature, man or beast, at will, and also to become invisible. He needed good luck, however, as well as courage, otherwise he was liable to be destroyed or damaged by demons during the collecting process. But few, it seems, attempted it, because of the risk to the health or the soul of the person concerned, and this, perhaps, was just as well.

When the great bonfires roared on hills and open spaces in the country, the people danced round them, and young men and girls leapt through them for strength and good fortune. The cattle, too, were driven over the embers to protect them from disease. In the Isle of Man, bonfires used to be built on the windward side of the fields, so that the fertilizing smoke should blow over the crops. In Cornwall, where there were many fires at this time, especially in the western part of the county, many of the Penwith parishes also had tar barrels flaming on the tops of long poles along the main streets of towns or villages. In Penzance, young men from the quayside marched through the town carrying torches made of canvas dipped in tar, and attached to chains by which they were swung, with great dexterity, round the bearers' heads, until they finally burned away. After that had happened, everyone fell to dancing in the streets, and playing Thread the Needle until fatigue and the coming of midnight drove them all home to bed.

Most of the Midsummer fires had died away by the end of last century, but the Federation of Old Cornwall Societies has revived many of the Cornish ones. A chain of great bonfires now burns again on St John's Eve, flaming across the county like war beacons of old. The ceremony of lighting these fires is carried through in the Cornish language. At Whalton, in Northumberland, there is another traditional fire which has needed no revival in our own day, or for at least two or three centuries back, and probably much more. The bonfire is lit on the village green, and the old tradition of dancing round it and leaping through it is still kept up. But the most interesting thing about this custom is its date, for it is held on the evening of 4 July, which is Midsummer Eve, Old Style. The calendar change in 1752, which altered the date of so many traditional festivals, passed over the heads of the Whalton people, apparently, and they continue, as of old, to celebrate their ancient ceremonies on Old Midsummer Eve.

The same thing seems to have happened at Appleton Thorn, in Cheshire, where the custom known as Bawming the Thorn is observed (though now somewhat intermittently) on 5 July, Old Midsummer Day. The dialect word *bawming* means adorning, or anointing, and refers in this case to the decoration with garlands, posies, flags and ribbons of the thorn tree which grows in the centre of the village, and gives it the latter half of its name. Tradition says that such a tree has grown there for rather more than eight centuries, the first having been planted by Adam de Dutton in 1125. It is said to have been an offshoot of the Holy Thorn of Glastonbury, a belief which is supposed to account for the reverence paid to it. In fact, however, it is far more likely that here we have a memory of ancient tree-worship. At the moment, the existing thorn is still young, its predecessor having been blown down in 1965, and this one planted in its place in 1967.

In the eighteenth and nineteenth centuries, and probably earlier, the garlanded tree was the centre, every year, of a little rural fête, many people coming from outside the village to see it and pay their respects to it. More than once, the custom was allowed to lapse, partly because the visiting crowds became rowdy and over-noisy, and sometimes damaged the property of the Appleton residents. But it was always revived after the passage of some time. It was so revived, slightly altered, in 1906, and again in 1930. In its present form, it consists of a procession of children through the village, the adornment of the tree, and dancing round it in a wide ring, singing, and after the ritual ceremonies are over, sports and games and jollifications of various kinds, and a festival tea for the dancers.

On 24 June, being St John's Day, a sermon is annually preached at Magdalen College, Oxford, from a stone-canopied pulpit in the first quadrangle. This commemorates the fact that an ancient hospital of St John the Baptist once stood on this site, its buildings passing into the hands of William Wayneflete when he founded Magdalen College in 1458. At one time the quadrangle was fenced with green boughs when the sermon was preached, in memory of St John's sojourn in the wilderness, but this custom was given up long ago. The actual preaching of the Midsummer sermon ceased for many years during the nineteenth century, but it was revived in 1896.

Children in some parts of London still celebrate Grotto Day on 25 July, which is the Feast of St James the Great, or on any of the days that follow up to, and including 5 August, which is Old St James's Day. They make little grottoes, usually of oyster shells (though really it ought to be scallop shells), stones and earth or clinkers from the gas works, and adorn them with small flowers and bits of coloured china or glass. Frequently there is a lighted candle inside the grotto itself. These little structures, when complete, are set up on street pavements, against the walls of buildings. Their makers stand beside them, cap in hand, and ask for pennies from the passers-by. ' A penny for the Grotto!' they cry, or ' Please to remember the Grotto!', or in districts where memories are longer, they repeat the old rhyme,

> Please to remember the Grotto,
> It's only once a year.
> Father's gone to sea,
> Mother's gone to fetch him home,
> So please remember me.

This custom seems to be declining now, and perhaps before very long, it will have vanished altogether from the London scene. But it has had a very long run. Once it was much more widespread than it is at present, extending over most of the nearer villages outside London, and even, at one time, as far as Brighton. Its roots run back to the Middle Ages, to the days when the great pilgrimages were made to the shrines of saints like that of St James of Compostella in Santiago. St James was the Apostle who brought the Gospel to Spain, and was afterwards beheaded in Jerusalem by Herod Agrippa in AD 44. His emblem was the scallop shell, which those who visited his shrine used to wear as a proof that they had been there. Legend says that, after his execution, his headless body was brought back to Spain and buried there. As the boat neared the coast, a rider on the shore plunged into the sea and swam towards it. He and his horse were saved from drowning only by the power of the saint, but when they emerged from the water, both were thickly covered by scallops. Henceforward the scallop shell became the acknowledged badge of St James which, from then on, appeared on carvings and statues, in pictures and embroideries everywhere, and should by rights appear now in the children's grottoes also. Sometimes it does – but oyster shells are so much easier to come by when you are still rather young, and have to depend upon the generosity of restaurant cooks and fishmongers.

The lovely custom of well-dressing flourishes in the flowery season of high summer, mainly in Derbyshire, though it is known also in Staffordshire, Gloucestershire, and elsewhere. The dressing of wells and springs on festival occasions runs back into remote antiquity and, in one form or another, is practically universal; but the way in which it is now done in Derbyshire does not seem to be known in any other country, and even in that limited region, dates only from last century. Until about 1818, the wells were all adorned in the ancient manner, with wreaths and garlands and flowers thrown into the water, but in that year, the first of the clay-covered boards are recorded, and the first ancestor of today's beautiful flower pictures appeared.

These pictures are usually religious in subject, with some reference to water. They are made by pressing petals (in some parishes, complete flower heads), leaves, grasses, mosses, tree cones, berries, and bark on to a design traced upon a large wooden screen covered with soft moist clay. Certain strict rules govern the selection of the materials. Everything used in the picture itself, or in the surrounding frame, has to be of natural origin, a rule which allows the use of small shells, or coloured pebbles, or rice, or dried peas, but not any manufactured article such as pieces of glass or of tin. The work, from the collection and preparation of the materials to the designing and making of the picture, and its erection by the well concerned (or sometimes by the tap that has replaced that well) is all done by local men most of whom have been doing it for years, and are quite often the sons or grandsons of other men who followed the same lovely craft in years gone by.

The best-known of the well-dressings is that at Tissington, where the five wells are dressed and blessed every year on Ascension Day. Tradition says that the custom of dressing the springs in thanksgiving for the gift of water began as far back as 1615, after a very severe and lengthy drought which had afflicted the whole county. There was no rain for weeks together, springs and small streams dried up everywhere; the parish clerk at Winster

records in his register that ' the greatest part of the land was
burnt up, both corn and hay '. But in Tissington, the five wells
continued to flow without abatement all through the rainless
period, supplying not only the needs of the villagers, but also
those of men and animals from other parishes who came seeking
water from far around. There is, however, another tradition which
puts the beginning of the thanksgiving custom much farther back,
to 1350, after the appalling devastation of the Black Death had
killed 77 out of the hundred priests in Derbyshire, and an
untold number of the laity. In the whole county, Tissington
alone is said to have escaped without a single death, an immunity
which the people ascribed to the Grace of God and the purity of
their wells. We cannot tell for certain now which, if either, of
these two tales is true, but it is quite possible that they both are.
We know that the well-dressing custom has lapsed and been
revived more than once in the course of time, and their escape
from the drought in 1615 may well have inspired the parishioners to revive a lapsed form of thanksgiving which had once
more become extremely appropriate. Today, the five wells are all
dressed every Ascension Day, each with its vividly coloured,
glowing flower picture set up behind it, and are visited by a
procession of clergy, choir and parishioners, a little service of
thanksgiving and blessing being held at each one.

Buxton has no such traditions to account for its well-dressing,
which takes place annually on the Thursday nearest to Midsummer Day. It is usually said to have begun about 1840, after
the then Duke of Devonshire had brought water to be piped into
the Market Place. Unlike those of Tissington, its well ceremonies
are not primarily religious (though the two wells of the town
are blessed), but, at least since 1947, have been the centre of a
very gay town festival, in which the mayor and corporation
take part, and over which a young Wells Festival Queen presides.
What is perhaps most interesting is not so much the modern
celebration as the long history of its famous St Ann's Well. This
is a warm medicinal spring which was known to the Romans,
and resorted to by them. Roman remains have been found near
it, and in 1709, during some alterations, the well itself was seen
to be lined with Roman lead and surrounded by Roman bricks.
At some rather uncertain period in the Middle Ages, the statue
of a woman was discovered in its depths, and was taken by the
local people to represent St Ann, though there is no known legend

connecting her with this district. It has been suggested that it may have been a Roman statue, perhaps representing a pagan water deity; but whether it was so or not, it was forthwith accepted as St Ann, to whom many miracles of healing were afterwards attributed.

At the time of the Reformation, Sir William Bassett, one of Thomas Cromwell's agents, came to Buxton, and finding the well and the adjacent chapel frequented by large numbers of sick and ailing people, promptly removed the statue, and sealed up the well and the chapel, so that no one could use them any more. This he did, as he wrote to his master, ' that there should be no more idolatry and superstition there used '. This was in 1538. By 1572, the well was open again and Buxton had become a fashionable spa. Three hundred years later, that well and its companion, the Higher Buxton Well, were being dressed, not yet with screen pictures, but with garlands and flags, and a Maypole. Almost certainly Sir William would have disapproved of this; but it is just possible that it may not have been the first of such ceremonies that the old well had known. We cannot altogether ignore that the possibility that in Roman times, or during the Middle Ages, well rituals may have been performed here, and offerings made, to the unknown pagan in-dweller of the spring, perhaps, or later, to St Ann, the loved grandmother of Our Lord.

Well-dressing at Wirksworth began with tap-dressing about 1827, when water was first brought down from the moor in wooden pipes, and stand cocks were set up in about seven different parts of the town. The taps were dressed with as much care as the springs were elsewhere, originally on the Wednesday in Whit Week, and later on Whit Monday, or Whit Saturday. Now the stand cocks have all been taken away, but the tap-dressings are still erected on the traditional sites. The pictures here are amongst the finest in the county, great stress being always laid upon the rules governing the nature of the materials used. There is, also, as at Buxton, a Wells Queen.

One other long-lived summer custom – rush-bearing – must be mentioned here, if only because traces of this once useful and necessary practice still exist in several parishes. When church floors were normally made of beaten earth, or at best, covered with stone flags, it was necessary to overcome the penetrating cold that rose from them by covering them with a thick carpet of rushes. These were renewed, as a rule, once a year (though occasionally oftener), usually at the time of the Wakes, when the bringing-in of the new reeds – the actual rush-bearing – was the great event of the day. They were ceremonially conveyed, sometimes carried by young women dressed in white, but far more usually piled upon a great harvest wain, decorated with flowers and ribbons and drawn by the finest horses in the parish, the towering load being held in place by flowered ropes and by the tall harvest-gearing. Morris dancers went before the rush cart, and sometimes young people walked beside it, carrying garlands which they afterwards hung up in the church; occasionally a bower of oak boughs was built on the top of the load, in which sat a man who directed the proceedings. In many parishes, it was customary for the rush procession to go all round the township, stopping outside the greater houses, where the Morris dancers performed; but eventually the rush cart and all its attendants reached the Church Town where, to the loud pealing of the bells, the reeds were pulled from it, and strewn all over the floor of the church.

The steady increase of wooden floors in churches during the eighteenth and nineteenth centuries gradually did away with the need for carpets of rushes. Nevertheless, the colourful and well-loved custom of rush-bearing continued for a long time, and there are still traces of it in a number of places today. One of the most famous surviving ceremonies is at Grasmere, in Westmorland. Here ' surviving' seems to be the right word, for the local people assert that the celebration has never been omitted, though the day on which it is held was changed in 1885 from the Saturday nearest 20 July to the Saturday nearest 5 August, the Feast of St Oswald, who is the patron saint of the parish church. There is no cart here, but the rushes are carried about in procession, either loose, in a hand-woven linen sheet borne by six young girls, or in separate ' rush-bearings ' – that is, reeds twisted into traditional shapes and figures. These figures include harps, crosses, Maypoles, gates, serpents on poles, Moses in a reed basket, and most especially St Oswald's crown, and his wonder-working Hand.

This is the Hand that St Aidan blessed because of its owner's great generosity to the poor, praying, at the same time, that it might never perish. Nor did it, according to tradition. After St Oswald's death in battle, it was preserved in a shrine at Bamburgh, where it remained, uncorrupted, for many years, until it was eventually stolen by a monk of Peterborough. Where it is now is unknown, and probably it was destroyed during the upheavals of the Reformation, but in its green and living form it is remembered every year at the Grasmere Rush-bearing. The ceremonies of that day include a procession round the village, headed by the clergy and a band, after which there is a church service. The rush-bearings are carried inside, and laid along temporary shelves all round the building. They are left there until the following Monday, and then their owners fetch them away, and there is another procession down to the School Field for tea and sports. At the end of the service on the Saturday, all the children are given pieces of ginger bread stamped with St Oswald's name.

Ambleside also has its traditional rush-bearing on the Saturday nearest St Anne's Day (26 July). Here, too, various devices made of rushes are carried in procession through the street, with flower garlands, and two great rush pillars about 10ft high, or more. There is a service in the church and after it, as at Grasmere, the children receive pieces of gingerbread bearing St Oswald's name. In two other Westmorland villages, Warcop and Great Musgrove, there are long-established rush-bearing customs on 29 June, but in the course of time, these seem to have become flower ceremonies rather than the real rush-carrying they once were. There is a quite charming procession of little girls wearing high garland crowns, made of light wood completely covered with flowers. The crowns are traditional, and were worn in the parish more than a century ago. There are also boys carrying rush crosses, but these crosses are modern, having been introduced about forty years ago by the vicar of that time, so that the people of the parish might remember the true origin of their rush-bearing anniversary. Garlands and rush crosses alike are carried into the church at the time of the service, and are deposited there.

On Whit Sunday, rushes are strewn in the church of St Mary Redcliffe, in Bristol, and posies of flowers are laid in every seat. This is the day on which the Lord Mayor of Bristol comes in state to the church, and is received, with trumpets, by the Bishop of Bristol, and subsequently listens to a special sermon preached before him. All this is in accordance with the will of another Mayor of Bristol, one William Spenser, who in 1493 left money to pay for three sermons (now reduced to one), which were to be preached at Pentecost before the Mayor and people of the

G

town in St Mary Redcliffe church. Money was allotted for the
strewing of the church with rushes, and for the pealing of the
bells, but the posies on the seats seem to have been added at some
later time.

A modified form of rush-bearing still exists in a few other
parishes. At Tarvin, in Cheshire, rushes are strewn in July upon
the churchyard graves, and a few are taken into the church. At
Barrowden, in Rutland, reeds are brought in on St Peter's Eve,
and allowed to lie on the floor for a week. Grass is laid down at
Shenington, in Oxfordshire, on Trinity Sunday and the Sunday following, as new hay is at Glenfield in Leicestershire on
the Thursday after 6 July, and at Wingrave, near Aylesbury
on the last Sunday of June. Hay also is scattered in Old Weston
Church, Huntingdonshire, on the Sunday nearest 15 July, the Feast
of St Swithun.

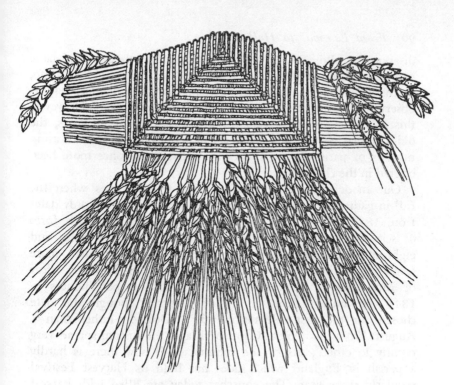

# 7 From Lammas to Hallowtide

THE FIRST DAY OF AUGUST is Lammas Day, which is a cross Quarter Day in England and a full Quarter Day in Scotland. It is also the day on which Lammas Lands that have been let to individuals during the summer revert to the community, and in a few districts, it is still one of the dates on which half-yearly rents fall due. The name Lammas is almost certainly derived from the Anglo-Saxon *Hlafmaesse*, or Loaf Mass, anciently the name of a festival of first-fruits held on this date when bread made from the first new corn of the year was offered in the churches. This was not a harvest festival, as we now understand that term, but a simple expression of gratitude for the ripening of the new corn, and the anniversary on which the bread of the Sacrament could first be made from it. This lovely old ceremony lapsed at some uncertain period in the later Middle Ages, and disappeared altogether after the Reformation, though the name survived. 'Lammas Day . . .', wrote P. H. Ditchfield in 1896, in his *Old English Customs*, ' remains in the calendar, but its observance as a feast of the first-fruits has passed away.' However, this is no longer quite true, for in the last 30 or 40 years, the old Lammas Service has been celebrated again in an increasing number of parishes, and the Lammas bread has once more been offered in the churches.

Our modern Harvest Thanksgiving, which comes when the full in-gathering is ended, is not at all old, and in fact, only dates from 1843. There does not seem to have been any such form of service in the Middle Ages, or during the seventeenth and eighteenth centuries, though of harvest rejoicings of a more secular kind there were plenty. The Rev. R. S. Hawker, Vicar of Morwenstow, in Cornwall, revived for his parishioners in 1843 the ancient thanksgiving of Lammas, though the date chosen for the first celebration was 1 October, rather than 1 August. From this remote Cornish village, the custom spread very rapidly to other parts of the country, until now there is hardly a parish in England which does not hold its Harvest Festival regularly every year. The churches today are filled with harvest gifts of all sorts – sheaves of corn, loaves, fruit, vegetables and flowers – all of them used to decorate the building for the festival, and destined thereafter for the local charities and hospitals. This is probably an addition since Hawker's time, but it is a very natural expression of harvest rejoicing. Certainly, this service has by now become immensely popular, in spite of its comparative newness; and it is sometimes said, quite probably with truth, that there are many people today who rarely go to church, but are always careful to be present at Christmas and at Harvest Festival.

Mechanization on the farm has swept away most of our oldest harvest customs, and has profoundly altered the appearance of the harvest field. Once, the latter was like Langland's ' fair field full of folk ', filled with casual labourers hired for the season, and, of course, all the men of the farm, most of whom brought their wives and their children with them, to help with the cutting and tying-up of the sheaves. Now, two or three men and a tractor are all that are left of that busy and cheerful throng. Formerly, in many parts of the country, there was a Lord and a Lady of the Harvest, chosen by their fellow workers to represent them, to bargain with the farmer, draw up the harvest rules, come first and second in the line, and to set the pace of the work. They have vanished with the hand-reaping, and so has that most cherished ritual, the cutting of the Last Sheaf, whose origins run back into remote antiquity. It was long considered to be unlucky to be the cutter of the last few stalks of standing corn, that last refuge of the Corn Spirit. Probably very few of the men knew exactly why it was unlucky, but most of them were reluctant to be the cutter. Consequently it was usual on many farms for the last stalks left standing to be tied or plaited together, and for all the men, gathered in a wide half-circle, to throw their sickles at them. Thus, the responsibility was shared amongst them all, and theoretically at least, no one could be accused of the final cutting.

Afterwards, on many farms, especially in the north and west, they Cried the Neck (or the Mare) that is, the Last Sheaf. The Harvest Lord, or some other respected person, held the Neck aloft, and shouted at the top of his voice: ' I havet! I havet! I havet!' All present then cried, ' What havee? What havee? What havee?', and the first man replied, ' A Neck! A Neck! A Neck!' All this, and the cheers and shouting that followed, were enough to let it be known over a considerable area that the harvest on that particular farm was nearly ended; but sometimes the men could not resist the temptation of mocking some neighbouring farmer who was behindhand with his cutting by the old and derisory ceremony known as Shutting. They all went to some piece of high ground overlooking the other man's unfinished fields, and shouted very loudly: ' Oyez! Oyez! Oyez! This is to give notice that Mr . . . (their own master) has given the Sack a turn, and sent the Old Hare into Mr . . . (the neighbour)'s standing corn!' Then, taking hands, they bowed down in a circle, and cried out ' Wow . . . wow . . . wow-w-w!' at the full strength of their lungs. This was a joke in the last years of the custom, but in earlier times, it had a more sinister meaning, for the Old Hare brought ill-luck with it, and the farm on which it was driven to seek its last refuge could expect only misfortune in the coming year.

The Last Load of the harvest – the Horkey Load in East Anglia – was brought home with great ceremony, piled up in a great wagon decorated with flowers and oak and ash boughs, and held in place by high harvest gearing. Four, or six, horses drew it, with garlands round their necks, and scarlet ribbons on their harness. The men rode on the top of the load, shouting and singing, and blowing horns, and the girls ran alongside and threw water over them all. On some farms, the driver of the wagon, or the men who rode the horses, were dressed as women. That night, the Harvest (or Mell, or Horkey) Supper was usually held in a barn or shed, which was cleaned out for the occasion and adorned with garlands of flowers. Everyone connected with the harvest was present, and all feasted upon roast beef or mutton, vegetables, plum pudding and apple pie, and a vast amount of ale or cider. Traditional songs were sung, toasts were proposed to the farmer and his family, and he in his turn drank to the men and thanked them for their work. At the end of it all, there was dancing. Mell or Harvest Suppers are still held in many farms today, though they are no longer quite the noisy, cheerful gatherings that they used to be. But they do, nevertheless, represent the survival of a very ancient custom, and of the old sense of shared triumph which once marked the harvest as the crown of the agricultural year.

When the Last Load was carried home, the figure known as the Corn Dolly, or the Kern Baby, was carried home with it, to preside over the Mell Feast, and to hang in the farm kitchen throughout the coming year. It was made from the corn of the Last Sheaf, and was a symbol of the Corn Spirit; while it was kept, it was a magical guarantee of harvests to come. It could be made in a variety of forms, sometimes in intricate designs of knots and braided loops, or a small sheaf, but perhaps most often as a female doll dressed in stiff coloured paper, and with hair and hands made of wheat-ears. In Little Waltham, in Essex, and at Whalton in Northumberland, Kern-Babies in doll-form are still brought every year to the parish church, and set up there as part of the Harvest Festival decorations. At Overbury, in Worcestershire, a twisted spiral of corn, with wheat ears hanging from its base, hangs in the church porch, and is renewed, not every year as in the other two villages, but when it becomes necessary. Of late years, there has been a remarkable revival in the art of making decorative corn dollies, an art now often taught in Women's Institutes, or in the village centres. Many fine designs are used, and very interesting figures produced; but the fact remains that they are purely ornamental, and no longer have their ancient meaning.

The old Corn Dolly, made on the field at the height of the harvest, and brought home with rejoicing for the protection of the homestead and the rickyards, is seen now no more.

A curious custom, which may once have had some connection with the harvest, is observed at West Witton, in Yorkshire. This is the Burning of Bartle, which now takes place on the Saturday nearest St Bartholomew's Day (24 August), but formerly was celebrated on St Bartholomew's Day itself, the patronal festival of the parish. An effigy, life-size, or even larger, is made every year and carried round the village. Wherever any house door has been left open, there the procession halts, Bartle is displayed to those within, and the bearers chant:

> At Pen Hill crags, he tore his rags,
> At Hunter's Thorn, he blew his horn,
> At Capplebank Stee, he brak his knee,
> At Grassgill Beck, he brak his neck,
> At Waddam's End, he couldn't fend,
> At Grassgill End, he made his end.

In the same way, if any car or bus is encountered on the route, Bartle is lifted up to its windows, and shown to the travellers. Finally, following the rhyme, he comes to his end at Grassgill End, where the effigy is thoroughly soaked in paraffin, and thrown upon a bonfire. Hidden fireworks go off all round him, the people shout, and then fall to singing popular songs, and Bartle burns away to ashes.

Who he was originally, and why he should be thus sacrificed every year, is not at all clear. Some say he was simply St Bartholomew, West Witton's patron saint, and that the bonfire is explained by some vague connection with the massacre of the Huguenots on the eve of his festival in 1572. Another story speaks of a swine thief in the neighbourhood (or, in another version, of a cattle-stealing giant), who was caught and killed, – though not by fire – by the indignant people of the parish. A third theory maintains that Bartle was never a human being, good or bad, but was originally a harvest deity, associated with fertility and good fortune, whose special day, falling in the harvest season, happened, in later years, to coincide with the Feast of St Bartholomew.

Painswick Feast is held on the Sunday nearest 19 September, the Feast of the Nativity of Our Lady according to the Old Style. On that day, the people of this Gloucestershire parish clip their church. The children walk there in procession and, holding hands, encircle the building, going towards it and retreating from it three times. The 'Clipping Hymn' is sung, and afterwards, a sermon is preached from a doorway in the tower to a crowd assembled in the churchyard.

This is not by any means the only parish in which this ancient dancing ceremony is, or has been, performed. Normally, it is a spring celebration, performed at Easter or at Shrovetide, but sometimes, as at Painswick, it is connected with the patronal festival. Two very curious customs, one obsolete and the other still in existence, are associated with the ceremony there. Formerly, at the end of the service, the children used to rush along the road towards the old vicarage, shouting 'Highgates! Highgates!' as they ran. No one knew the meaning of this word, and today this part of the celebration has vanished. There is also the making of puppy-dog pies, which still goes on. On Clipping Day, housewives make 'pies', which are really round cakes with a ring of almond paste on their tops, and a small china dog inside. Tradition says that originally, these were real pies containing genuine dog-meat.

At the end of last century, the Rev. W. H. Seddon, then Vicar of the parish, produced a pamphlet called *Painswick Feast*, in which he made some interesting suggestions concerning the origin of the 'puppy-dog pies' and of the word 'Highgates'. He believed that the clipping festival was of Roman origin, and could be traced back through the centuries to the pagan feast of the *Lupercalia*. This was essentially a festival of youth, and must have been known in the neighbourhood, in the days when Painswick was a Roman settlement. It included a sacred dance round an altar, the sacrifice of goats and young dogs, and a wild rush of young men, the *Luperci*, who performed the sacrifice through the streets, shouting, and striking all the women they met with goat-skin thongs. Mr Seddon thought that the children's rush to the vicarage might spring from a vague memory of this ritual, and that the word 'Highgates' which they shouted on their way might be a corruption of the Greek *aig-aitis*, from *aig*, a goat, and *aitis*, an object of love. He believed also that the 'puppy-dog pies', with their tradition of real dog-meat formerly, were probably derived from the dog sacrifice of the *Lupercalia*.

On the Monday following the first Sunday after 4 September, that is, the Monday in the local Wakes Week, the ancient Horn Dance is danced every year in the Staffordshire village of Abbot's Bromley. Once, it seems to have been a winter solstice ritual, and Robert Plot, in his *Natural History of Staffordshire* (1686) speaks of it as being performed at Christmas, on New Year's Day, and at Twelfth Night. We know, also, that at one time it was danced outside the church every Sunday, and that alms were collected after the performance for the parish poor. No one knows how old it is, but obviously, from the nature of the dance itself, it is exceedingly ancient, and has its beginnings in pre-Christian times.

The team of performers includes six men, wearing horns, who are the centre of the whole celebration, a Fool, in motley, a Man–Woman, known as Maid Marian, who wears a long dress and a veil, and carries a wooden ladle for collecting money, a Hobby-Horse with movable jaws, a Bowman, a boy with a triangle, and a musician. The Fool and the Man–Woman wear their own special costumes, but all the rest of the company are dressed in knee-breeches, flat caps, knitted green stockings, and brightly coloured sleeveless jerkins. This is not traditional, though it is fast becoming so. Formerly, the men wore their own clothes, decorated with ribbons and patches of coloured cloth, until, during the latter half of last century, some ladies of the parish made a set of costumes slightly reminiscent of those shown in the Betley Window – and these rather charming garments have been repeated and renewed as necessary from then on.

The horns worn by the six principal dancers are reindeer antlers, mounted upon carved wooden deer heads, and attached to short poles for carrying. Three are painted white and three blue (though at different periods we hear of different colours). They are carried in such a way that the great antlers seems to be springing from the men's own heads, and very striking they look as the dancers move with them through the traditional measures. The largest pair, which is always worn by the leader of the team, weighs over 25lb, and has a span of 39ins; the others vary in size and are lighter, but even so, the smallest weighs 16½lb, which is surely quite enough for anyone to carry round a parish extending over some 20 miles. How these alien horns came to be in Abbot's Bromley is unknown. Occasionally they are confused with a set of horns which Lord Paget is known to have brought home from Turkey at the end of the seventeenth century; but these were, in fact, elk horns and in any case, they seem to have been lost at some later period. Other suggestions are that they were imported by some early Norse settler in the district, or that they are actually of British origin, which would date them well before the twelfth century, since reindeer are believed to have been extinct in these islands by then. The horns are kept in the church, in the Hurst Chapel, and are fetched thence by the dancers on Wakes Monday before the ceremonies begin.

The dance itself is simple, and during the day, it is performed all over the scattered parish, outside all the farmhouses, cottages and other dwellings over a circle of more than 20 miles. It begins with a single-file ring that fades, following the leader into a serpentine loop. Then the horned men divide into two lines of three each, facing each other, advance, as though the reindeer were about to fight, and retire, repeating the movement several times, and finally crossing over, left shoulder to left shoulder, turning, and beginning all over again. Eventually they fall once more into single file, and follow the leader quietly away to whatever house or cottage is their next port of call. That they are luck-bringers is clear from the fact that it is thought to be very unlucky if they do not come to any dwelling. The full round of the parish takes up most of the day, and then the team returns to the village, to dance in the street there, and later to return the horns to the care of the church till they are needed again.

On the last Thursday in October, the children of Hinton St George, in Somerset, keep Punkie Night. A ' punkie ' is a lantern made from a mangel-wurzel, hollowed out, and elaborately adorned with designs of flowers, or animals, or ships, cut upon the outer skin. The inner pith is cut away, leaving only enough to maintain the lantern shape. Inside this homemade lantern a candle, begged from one of the householders during the days beforehand, is set. Traditionally, this annual request for candle ends is never refused, because it is supposed to be unlucky to do so. When dusk falls on the October anniversary, the children parade the streets with their lighted punkies, visiting the different houses, and singing as they go :

It's Punkie Night tonight.
Give us a candle, give us a light,
If you don't, you'll get a fright.

It's Punkie Night tonight,
Adam and Eve, they'd never believe
It's Punkie Night tonight.

Some years ago, before the outbreak of World War II, a well-meaning new policeman, unacquainted with the village and its traditions, tried to suppress the Punkie Night parades, in much the same way as another newcomer attempted to stop the Garland Day processions at Abbotsbury in 1964. In both places, the result was the same – a storm of adult protest, and an appeal to the Chief Constable of the county, by whom the unwelcome ban was at once lifted.

The origin of Punkie Night is not certainly known. There is a vague local tradition that it was once connected in some way with the now obsolete Chiselborough Fair, but it seems obvious that this little festival of lights, with its guiser-like lanterns, really belongs to the Hallow-tide circle. A somewhat similar custom is observed in a few other south Somersetshire villages, but in these the parades are not held on a fixed date, as at Hinton St George, but simply during the week in which Hallowe'en falls.

The short season of Hallow-tide, which consists of Hallowe'en on 31 October and All Saints and All Souls of 1 and 2 November, has been associated from time immemorial with fire and the cult of the dead. By the ancient calendar of the pagan Celts, the year and the winter began together on 1 November, and the old and splendid Feast of Samhain, or Summer's End, was also New Year's Eve. This was a time of games and sports, and of late harvest celebrations in the northern regions, of bonfires through which young men leapt, and of enquiries into the future by charms and divinations. Above all, it was the time when ghosts and strange spirits from the Underworld walked abroad, and the dead returned to their homes.

After the coming of Christianity, this pagan holy season was hallowed by the Church. In the ninth century, 1 November became the Feast of All Saints, and a century later, 2 November was made the Feast of All Souls. These were deeply Christian

festivals, as they still are, but they did not destroy all the beliefs
and traditions of the earlier time. The notion of the returning
dead lingered on everywhere until the Reformation, and was
never quite forgotten afterwards. In Roman Catholic countries,
where there was no upheaval of belief and practice, it lasted
much longer. The great Hallow fires – the *teanlas*, tandles, or
tindles of country naming – continued to blaze upon hill-tops and
open spaces right down to the end of the nineteenth century, as
five days later, and under another name, they still do in the form
of Guy Fawkes Night bonfires. In Lancashire and Westmorland, and also in Derbyshire, a farmer would sometimes light
a small fire of his own in one of his fields, and when it was
burning well and fiercely, would take a mass of flaming straw
from it upon a pitchfork and carry it up to the highest point of
the ground. There he flung it as far as he could over the land,
to purify the soil and guard it against evil, and to make the
crops grow in due course. Meanwhile his family knelt round
the bonfire and remembered the dead of their kin. Whether they
actually prayed for them or not presumably depended upon
their particular form of religion, but there is no doubt that this
was the original intention of the custom, and that, prayers or
not, the ceremony was believed to help the dead. On some old
farms in the north, there are fields still known as Purgatory
Field, because once this ritual, half pagan and half Christian,
was performed there.

In Cheshire and Shropshire, small bands of children still go
Souling through the villages on All Souls' Day (or on All
Saints' Day which is its Eve). They visit the houses and sing
one or other of the traditional Souling-songs, and are then
rewarded with gifts of money, or cakes, or sweets. Formerly,
every housewife baked quantities of light, sweet cakes, known as
Soul-cakes, or small round loaves of Soul-bread, all specially
made to be given to the Soulers, or to anyone else who came
to the house that day; but this custom is forgotten now.

Until the second half of the last century, it was not children, but young men, and often their elders, who went round
Souling. In Cheshire, they were frequently accompanied by
the Hodening Horse, a man covered by a white sheet, or a stable-
blanket, and wearing, or carrying upon a short pole, a horse's
head (usually a real horse skull) with hinged jaws. He was
known in other parts of England at Christmas or at Twelfth

Night, but in Cheshire, he always came out at Hallow-tide and went round with the Soulers. He pranced and capered outside the house-doors, while the Soulers stood round him and sang their ancient songs. Seen unexpectedly in the dusk of a November evening, he could be a very alarming creature, but he was, nevertheless, a bringer of good fortune to the houses he visited. He appeared also in the Soul-Caking Play, which is the Cheshire version of the old Mumming Play, and always acted in that county on All Souls' Night. It is the only form of the play which contains a character known as Wild Horse, who wears a horse's head. Before 1914, the Soul-Caking Play was regularly acted in several Cheshire villages, but after the end of World War I, the custom lapsed in many places. It is, however, still regularly performed at Antrobus, near Great Budworth – Wild Horse and all.

The fires that once blazed on Hallowe'en now burn on 5 November, on which date we remember – or at least, some of us do – the discovery of the Gunpowder Plot in 1605 and the subsequent execution of Guy Fawkes. Parliament, redeemed almost at the last moment from a violent and horrifying death, ordered that 5 November should be kept as a permanent holiday and general day of rejoicing, and the people responded with enthusiasm, so much so indeed, that, although this day is no longer a statutory holiday, it has become, through the centuries, the one great Festival of Fire still observed in this country. Guy Fawkes is burnt in effigy on this night (though, in fact, he was hanged); bonfires, with or without the central figure of a Guy, flame on countless open spaces and inside the boundaries of private gardens; fireworks are let off everywhere, and in many places there are splendid torchlight processions. At Rye, in Sussex, the Bonfire Boys drag a boat through the streets, and then burn it on the Town Flats, along with a fine collection of official orders and prohibitions torn off the walls.

In most regions, all this has become mainly ' fun and games ' but in Lewes, and also in Bridgwater, in Somerset, 5 November celebrations are still taken very seriously. In both these towns old religious animosities endured longer than in most places in the one because of the 17 local martyrs who perished there by fire during the reign of Mary I, in the other because of memories of the Bloody Assizes after Monmouth's rebellion. At one time, in Lewes, huge bonfires used to be lit within the town limits (instead of an open space outside them, as now), and flaming tar barrels used to be rolled through the roadways in a highly dangerous manner. In the nineteenth century, many fires and much damage forced the authorities to attempt to suppress the celebrations altogether, but the only result of their efforts was to provoke serious rioting, especially in 1847. Eventually, as a compromise, the control of the ceremonies, and the maintenance of law and order were undertaken by the six Bonfire Societies (and in Bridgwater, where there were similar difficulties, by the Committee), since when everything has worked well in both towns.

In Lewes, at the beginning of the proceedings, each of the Bonfire Societies comes in turn to the war memorial, where they deposit wreaths, sing hymns, and hear a short sermon. Thereafter follow torchlight processions, which go on from dusk until nearly midnight, and finally the burning of the effigies on the allotted place outside the town. The oldest of the six societies is the Cliffe Society, which possesses, and occasionally brings out, its famous No Popery banner, and its figure of Pope Paul IV, who is locally supposed to have been the real author and inspiration of the Plot.

Ottery St Mary, in east Devon, has its own spectacular method of celebrating Guy Fawkes Night, a method which is probably unique in this country now, though something rather like it was known in other parishes in former times. Nine blazing tar barrels are carried, or rolled, along a fixed route, the first barrel being set alight at 8.15 at night outside the Factory, and the rest following in due course as the earlier ones are burnt out. As soon as the first barrel is well and truly burning, a man with his hands and arms swathed in thick sacking, picks it up and, holding it well above his head, runs with it as far as he can down the street. When he can no longer bear the intense heat, he puts it down and lets it roll along the road until another man seizes it and carries it forward till he, too, is overcome. When it becomes too hot for anyone to hold, it is rolled onwards until finally it vanishes in a sheet of flames. In turn, each barrel is transported by intrepid men, and allowed to roll along until, at a little before midnight, the last of the eight reaches the end of its course. The evening ends with the burning of a Guy on a massive bonfire. This splendid, fiery custom is the pride of the parish, and it is not likely to die out for some time yet. Every year, at four o'clock on 5 November, there is a kind of junior rehearsal when boys, swathed in sacking like their elders of the evening run about with four or five lighted barrels, and so learn to be as tough and as impervious to burns as the men whose places they will one day take in the main celebration.

An odd ceremony, which clearly has nothing to do with the Gunpowder Plot, and had its beginnings a very long time before James I and Guy Fawkes were ever thought of, takes place regularly at Shebbear, in North Devon, on 5 November. In this village there is a large stone known as the Devil's Boulder which lies just outside the east gate of the churchyard, and is supposed to have been either accidentally dropped by Satan, or deliberately brought there by him from Henscott, when the people of this latter village were intending to use it as a foundation stone for their new church. In fact, it appears to be an ' erratic ', one of those boulders of alien geological type which the re-treating ice at the end of the Ice Age left behind in various places. Once a year, the bell-ringers ' turn the Devil's Boulder ' with crowbars, after sounding a jangled peal on the church bells. It is said to be very unlucky to omit this ritual in any year, and liable to bring misfortune on the parish; but exactly why it has to be performed on this particular date is not clear. One trad-itional explanation is that, when Henscott was trying to build its church, the Devil removed the foundation stone and carried it to Shebbear so many times that the Henscott people grew tired of fetching it back, and one day, they quietly left it there. That day was 5 November. Since then, it has been left untouched, except once a year, when the bell-ringers come with their crowbars and lighted torches and, watched over by the majority of the parishioners, solemnly turn it over.

In parts of the Midlands and northern England, especially in Yorkshire, Guy Fawkes Eve (4 November) is Mischief Night, when a kind of licensed lawlessness prevails among the young people, and every sober householder is careful to lock away all his portable and easily come-at possessions, and to ignore every attempt to make him come to his door, or look out of the window. Outside, fireworks flare and rockets soar, and every kind of prank is practised by hilarious young people. Door knobs are smeared with treacle, or one may be tied to that of the house next door, with the result that neither door will open. House numbers are sometimes unscrewed and exchanged with others – to the great confusion of visitors or postmen next day –

smouldering papers are stuffed into drainpipes, windows are daubed with paint or whitewash. A favourite trick is to remove gates and carry them off to be hidden in ditches or other convenient spots, or thrown into ponds. Looking for lost gates, and rehanging them when found, is one of the normal tasks of householders on the morning after 4 November.

All this is more or less tolerated by the people of the district, in spite of a few grumbles and letters to the newspapers, because Guy Fawkes Eve is Mischief Night, and young people are traditionally allowed to run wild then. But in fact, the original Mischief Night was Hallowe'en (or in some areas, May Eve), and it was only towards the end of the nineteenth century that it became part of the Guy Fawkes celebrations. In some parts of Devon, it still is Hallowe'en, or was until very recently, and in the Calder Valley of Yorkshire, something rather like it is occasionally observed on May Eve. But for most people, Mischief Night has now quite definitely become part of the Guy Fawkes cycle, at least in a wide region stretching from Derbyshire to the north of Yorkshire.

One other custom connected with the discovery of the Gunpowder Plot may be mentioned here, though this is a State ceremony rather than a folk custom. Before the Opening of Parliament, usually in the morning of the day itself, but sometimes on the night before, a detachment of the Yeomen of the Guard comes from the Tower of London to the Palace of Westminster, and there carries out a prolonged and thorough search of all the basements, vaults, galleries, corridors, and every conceivable place where it would be possible to conceal barrels of gunpowder or, more probably in these days, a powerful bomb. They carry candle lanterns, notwithstanding the existence of a very effective electric-lighting system, and with these, they peer diligently into every nook and cranny. When, by the most rigorous personal inspection, they have satisfied themselves that all is well, a message is sent to the Queen, and the preparations for the Opening of Parliament can then proceed without anxiety. It need hardly be said that this is not the only precaution taken against the possible action of the Queen's enemies on this special occasion; but notwithstanding its traditional character, the search made by the Yeomen of the Guard is an exceedingly strict one, which any secret conspirators would find it extremely hard to elude.

# 8 Civic Customs

SOME OLD AND COLOURFUL CUSTOMS belong essentially to a particular town or community because they sprang, originally, from some part of the local history, or from some deep-seated local tradition. Such a custom is the splendid civic festival known as Preston Guild, which takes place, once in every 20 years, at Preston, in Lancashire. It begins in the week following the secondary feast of St John the Baptist, that of his martyrdom (29 August), and runs on for a further week thereafter. During that time, the Guild Court meets, the Guild Mayor, the Masters and Wardens of the Companies, and the burgesses walk in procession to the Parish Church, to hear a special sermon preached, and besides various other processions, there are balls, concerts, receptions, a fair, and every kind of entertainment.

All this began as a customary meeting of Preston's medieval Guild Merchant, which is believed to have existed by prescriptive right before the town received its first charter. The medieval guilds were extremely powerful institutions, exercising a strong

H

authority over every aspect of the local trade and commerce, endowing its members with a number of privileges, and above all, providing them with a virtual monopoly in all their trading. No outsider was allowed to trade within the town limits without permission, except, of course, at the time of the fairs. In the document known as the *Custumale of Preston*, usually said to be of twelfth-century date, it is stated that among ' the liberties of Preston in Amundernesse ', there shall be ' a Guild Merchant with Hanse and other customs, and belonging to such a Guild; and so that no one who is not of that Guild shall make any merchandize in the said town, unless with the will of the burgesses ', Charles Hardwick, *Histoy of Preston* (1857). Every guild town barred outside strangers except during a fair, but Preston seems to have been particularly prejudiced against them. As late as the seventeenth century they were strongly disliked, not only as traders, but also as lodgers or temporary residents. In 1616, a bylaw was passed, whereby any stranger lodging with a householder of the town, or sharing his house, might be considered by the town council, to be ' noe fitte person to inhabitte ' the borough, in which case he had to leave within a month of having notice served upon him; and if he did not, the householder concerned had to pay a weekly fine of 6s 8d until he did.

Preston Guild was not fixed at 20-year intervals until 1562. Before then, it seems to have been held irregularly, beginning, so far as clear records tell us, in 1329, and being repeated in 1397, 1415, 1459, 1501, 1543, and 1562. Since the last-named date, however, it has been regularly held every 20 years, except in 1942, when it had to be postponed on account of the war then raging. It was held ten years later, in 1952, and again in 1972, and it may be confidently expected once more in 1992.

Nevertheless, there was a time when it seemed in considerable danger of coming to an end. In the course of years, some of the older privileges of the Freemen had vanished for various reasons, and with the passing of the Municipal Reform Act in 1835, the last traces of the Guild Merchant's old authority and power were swept away. The next Preston Guild after the passing of the Act fell due in 1842, and there was a great deal of argument as to whether, in the new circumstances, it was worthwhile to hold it then, or indeed, ever again. After much discussion, it was finally decided to continue in the old way, though as a con-

cession to the losing side in the debate, the length of the festival
was reduced from the customary fortnight to a week. Now, at the
meeting of the Guild Court, after the charters granted to the
borough at various times have been read, a roll-call of all the
Free Burgesses is called, and the new Freemen are admitted. To
be a Freeman may not now carry the many trading privileges
that once it did, but it is still a distinction of which the holders
are normally extremely proud.

At Lichfield, a festival commonly called the Greenhill (or
Lichfield) Bower and Court of Array takes place annually in late
May or June, at one time on Whit Monday but now, like so many
other events of the same kind, on the new Spring Holiday. This
is really two customs, of which the first – the Bower – is said to
run back to the time of King Oswy of Northumbria, who con-
quered Mercia in the seventh century, and founded the Lichfield
bishopric in AD 656. It may be even older than King Oswy's
time, and perhaps began as a pagan celebration connected with
midsummer. It seems from the beginning to have been a festival
of flowers and greenery. In the Middle Ages, the city guilds used
to meet at Greenhill on Whit Monday, carrying flower garlands
and emblems of their trades. Now the Bower ceremonies have
become a sort of carnival, wherein lorries carrying tableaux, trade
floats, decorated carts, and bands pass cheerfully through streets
profusely adorned with flowers and greenery.

The second part of the custom is the meeting of the Court of
Array and the inspection of the ancient suits of armour which the
city was once obliged by law to provide. By an Act passed in
1176, and again by the Statute of Winchester in 1285, every
freeman between the ages of 15 and 60 had to keep a sufficiency
of arms and armour (varying in type and quantity according to
his standing), and maintain them in good condition and ready for
use. He had also to be able to handle them efficiently himself. In
addition, every county had to have its Commissioners of Array
whose duty it was to see that these regulations were duly carried
out by the freemen, and to hold periodical inspections of the
weapons and suits of armour provided by them. Such a Court of
Array existed in Lichfield, and seems from an early date to have
held its meetings on the same day as, and closely associated with,
the ancient Greenhill Bower.

The Court met, as it still does, at the Guildhall, and at once
adjourned to Greenhill. Here stood the Bower, a leafy erection of

green branches, which probably started life as one of those long
' summer halls ' often set up for dancing and merriment at Whitsun and other festivals. Here the householders of the various
wards were required to answer to their names, and here the
inspection of the arms took place. In the reign of James I, it ceased
to be legally necessary to hold Courts of Array, but Lichfield
continued to maintain theirs, and has gone on doing so down to
the present time. The city possesses a number of medieval suits
of armour, and these are brought out on Greenhill Bower Day,
and paraded, as of old, before the Sheriff and the members of the
Court.

In Lichfield also, the custom of the Sheriff's Ride is observed
every year on 8 September, the Feast of the Nativity of the
Blessed Virgin Mary, as it has been at least since Tudor times.
By a charter of that period, confirmed by Charles II in 1664, the
Bailiffs and Brethren of the city were obliged to elect, on 25 July,
a Sheriff chosen from amongst the citizens who were not already
Brethren. This man, in his turn, had to accept office, on pain of
fine or imprisonment, and the loss of civic privileges. One of his
duties was, and still is, to perambulate the city boundaries once
a year, accompanied as a rule, by 40 or 50 horsemen who go with
him for the whole of the 16-mile circle.

On the morning of 8 September, the cavalcade, after being
entertained by the Sheriff, leaves the Guildhall at about eleven
o'clock, and proceeds to encircle the city, halting at all the
ancient boundary marks, and at places where such marks formerly
stood. The whole round, allowing for stops along the route for
refreshments and formalities, takes most of the day, and it is
usually getting towards evening before they return. They are
met by the Sword- and Mace-bearers of the city, who ceremonially
conduct the Sheriff back to the Guildhall. This Riding is altogether a civic custom, and has nothing at all to do with the
ecclesiastical bound-beating on Ascension Day, which has already
been described.

On 1 September every year, the Mayor of Colchester and
the Town Clerk, together with some members of the Town
Council and of the Fishery Board, embark in a fishing-boat at
Brightlingsea, and sail out into Pyefleet Creek. Colchester is the
owner of all the oyster fisheries of the river Colne, which were
bestowed upon them by Richard I in 1186, and it is the right of
the Mayor to open the dredging season by making the first dredge

himself. The Town Clerk first reads aloud a Proclamation dated 1256, in which it is firmly stated that the fisheries in the Colne have belonged to Colchester ' from the time beyond which memory runneth not to the contrary '. Then the Queen's health is drunk in gin, and pieces of gingerbread are shared among the company; after which, the Mayor, wearing his civic robes and chain, solemnly lowers the trawl and brings up the first oysters of the new season.

A few weeks later, on or about 20 October, the famous Oyster Feast is held. Colchester used to be well-known for its civic feasts at one time, but these, since they were all held at the expense of the ratepayers, did not survive the ruthless cleaning-up activities of the Municipal Reform Act of 1835. The historic Oyster Feast was swept away then with the rest, but it was revived later, and has since been held annually on or about the traditional date. It has, in fact, grown in magnificence and importance, if anything, and usually has about 300 or 400 guests, often including some very distinguished personages from outside. It is said that more than 12,000 oysters are normally consumed on this festive occasion.

Round about 1180, Wakelin de Ferrers, whose ancestors had been Master of the Horse to the Dukes of Normandy, and had come over to England with William the Conqueror, built the castle at Oakham, and by way of asserting his territorial power and importance, he demanded that every peer of the realm, on coming for the first time to the Manor of Oakham, should forfeit a shoe from his horse, or else pay a sum of money in compensation to the bailiff. These shoes (or in the case of refusal, a substitute paid for by the compensation money) were originally nailed to the castle door, for all to see, but now they are kept indoors on the walls of the Great Hall. The majority of those to be seen there today are, in fact, substitutes, and many of them are of immense size and fanciful construction. All are marked with the name of the giver and the date on which he gave it.

This custom still survives. Most peers do cheerfully pay the required tribute on their first visit to Oakham, even though they rarely now arrive on horseback. The bailiff was originally empowered to seize a shoe by force if the visitor refused to give one, or to pay the fine, and presumably he still has that power today, at least theoretically. However, no one has put the matter to the test for a very long time, and the bailiff's right of seizure may possibly have lapsed through non-usage. De Ferrers, or his successors, did not scruple to demand his horseshoes from travelling royalty as well as from lesser men, though whether he actually had the right to do so, or the power to enforce the demand, is not clear. Queen Elizabeth I, when she was still a princess, duly paid her toll in 1556. Since then, a number of princes and reigning monarchs have done the same, including George IV when he was Prince Regent, Queen Victoria, Edward VII and George VI, the Duke of Windsor when he was Prince of Wales, and the Duke of Edinburgh. In 1967, Queen Elizabeth II, visited Oakham and presented a shoe.

At Ripon, in Yorkshire, the city horn is sounded every night at nine o'clock by the Mayor's Hornblower, who blows it first at four points in the Market Place, and then once outside the Mayor's house. This custom is locally said to run back to Anglo-Saxon times, and perhaps it does; certainly, it was in existence in 1400, except that it was not the Mayor's Hornblower who sounded the horn then, but the Wakeman, who was once the city's chief official. 'Unless Ye Lord Keep Ye Cittie, Ye Wakeman Waketh In Vaine', declares the civic motto, painted in large letters across the front of the town hall, a motto now shared by another Ripon, in Wisconsin, USA. The Wakeman formerly was responsible, among other things, for the protection of the citizens against robbery and violence during the night hours, and anyone who suffered loss or damage during that time could claim compensation from him, provided he could prove that such loss or damage was due to the negligence of the Wakeman, or that of his assistants. In addition to sounding the horn nightly, as a form of curfew, and also to announce the beginning of his official watch, he was required to sound it on the five Horn Days. These were originally kept on Candlemas Day, Easter, one of the Rogation days, St Wilfred's Day (12 October), and St Stephen's Day (26 December), but are now held on Easter Sunday, Whit Sunday, August Bank Holiday, Christmas Day, and Mayor's Sunday.

In 1604, Hugh Ripley, who was the last Wakeman of Ripon, became its first Mayor, and was no longer required to blow the city horn, as of old. An official Hornblower was appointed to relieve him of this part of his former duties. In 1955, on the resignation of Thomas Hawley, who had filled the post for many years, it was found necessary to duplicate the office, and appoint two Hornblowers instead of one, so that each might occasionally leave Ripon for a holiday, if he wished to do so. Until then, this had been impossible, since the Hornblower had to be on duty every night without fail, and always to be back from any outing in good time to put on his tricorne hat and long coat, and collect the horn, before nine o'clock.

The horn now used is the third that Ripon has possessed during the lifetime of this custom, and it is not very old, dating only from 1864. It replaced an older one which had been in use since 1690. The most ancient of the three, which is said to have been first blown in AD 886, is never sounded now, but it is carefully preserved among the city's most treasured possessions and is brought out on the five Horn Days, and other ceremonial occasions. It is carried then by the Sergeant-at-Mace, attached to a magnificent baldric which is adorned with heavy silver medallions depicting the arms and trades of former Wakemen and Mayors.

At Bainbridge, a village in Upper Wensleydale, there is another horn, which is blown every night at nine o'clock between Michaelmas Eve and Shrove Tuesday. In summer, it is silent because it is not needed, being intended as a guide to travellers lost, or in danger of being lost, on the high moors in the long, dark nights of winter. No one knows exactly how old this custom is, but it is undoubtedly very ancient, and is believed by some to run back to the time of the Romans.

The Woodmen of Arden hold their annual Wardmotes at Meriden, in Warwickshire, a parish which claims to be the real centre of England, and was very near the centre of the Forest of Arden, when that forest extended over a wide acreage in the Midlands. The Woodmen are a company of archers which was formed in 1785, a successor of many such companies which once existed in the forest in the days when archery was all-important. Membership is limited to 80 archers, and these wear a uniform of eighteenth-century style, consisting of a green coat with gilt buttons, buff waistcoat and white trousers, and a green hat. The bows used at the Wardmotes are 6ft yew bows, of the type used at Crecy and Agincourt, and the arrows are stamped with their weight in silver, as was the usual practice in the Middle Ages. There are three Wardmotes, at which the main archery competitions take place – one in June, one in July, and the Grand Wardmote, lasting for four days, which is held at the beginning of August.

The oldest sculling race in the world is the Thames Watermen's race for Doggett's Coat and Badge, which takes place annually on

1 August, or as near that date as the state of the tide will allow. In 1715, Thomas Doggett, a London actor-manager of strong pro-Hanoverian views, gave an orange-coloured coat and a silver badge showing the White Horse of Hanover, to be competed for by six young watermen who had completed their apprenticeship within the previous 12 months. This he did to mark, ' for ever ', as he said, the anniversary of George I's accession to the throne. When he died in 1721, he left money to perpetuate the race, and this is now administered on his behalf by the Worshipful Company of Fishmongers, who are also responsible for all the arrangements. The Fishmongers have added other awards to the original Coat and Badge, and now the winner of the race receives £10 in addition to Doggett's original bequest, and every competitor who actually reaches the winning post, even though late in the day, receives a prize. The course extends from London Bridge to Chelsea Bridge, and as the race is always rowed against the tide, it is a quite considerable test of endurance and skill. It is, however, very popular, and eliminating heats are usually necessary before the event to reduce the number of entrants to the permitted six. The Coat has now changed from orange to scarlet, and the boats used have become light outriggers instead of the much heavier craft of the founder's day; but otherwise the race has changed very little in the 260 years or thereabouts that have passed since its foundation.

On a day in early July, after the installation of their new Master and Warden, the members of the Worshipful Company of Vintners go in procession from their hall in Upper Thames Street to St James's, Garlickhithe, which is their parish church. They carry posies of sweet herbs in their hands, and before them go two Wine Porters in white smocks and top hats, carrying besoms with which they sweep a clear passage in the road before them. When the Company was young, in the days of King John, and for a long time after, both posies and besoms were very necessary, for medieval streets were shockingly ill-kept as a rule, and the stench which rose from the decaying garbage that householders carelessly threw into the roadway was quite appalling. The Vintners share with other companies the custom of standing in threes when the Loving Cup goes round at their banquets. One man stands to drink from the heavy cup, and the other two stand before and behind him, so that he would be fully protected in case of sudden attack. This custom is said to have arisen from the murder, in AD 978, of Edward the Martyr, who was treacherously stabbed outside Corfe Gate while drinking a farewell cup of wine.

The Vintners also share with the Dyers' Company the rare privilege of owning swans on the Thames. The only other swan-owner on the river is the Queen. The swan is a royal bird, and has always been so, and in earlier times, it could not be owned by any ordinary person unless the right to do so was expressly bestowed upon him by the Sovereign. Such a gift was a strong mark of royal favour, and carried with it a swan-mark whereby ownership could be indisputably recognized. In 1482, an Act of Parliament limited possession of a ' game of swans ' to holders of land or tenements of the yearly value of five marks or more. Today, anyone can keep captive birds on his own private waters, but any swans bearing no marks and found at large on open waters are automatically deemed to belong to the sovereign.

The Dyers received the right to keep swans in 1473, and the Vintners at some time between 1472 and 1483. Once a year, usually in the last week of July, they take part in the necessary work of Swan Upping, whereby all the young birds between London and Henley are caught, examined, and marked with the swan-marks of their owners. This is a laborious and quite strenuous process and usually takes several days. The Swanherds maintained by both Companies meet the Royal Swanherd at Southwark Bridge from whence all three, with their assistants, set out up-river in a procession of six rowing boats. First goes the Royal Swanherd's boat, flying two flags, and followed by another royal boat flying only one. These flags bear the Queen's initials and a crown on one, and on the other, a swan with raised wings. The Companies provide two boats, with one flag in each displaying swans and the arms of the Company concerned.

On their quite considerable journey, the Uppers have to catch, examine, and, where necessary, mark some 600 birds, some of which object strongly to the process. The adult birds (if they belong to the Companies) are already marked, and now the cygnets of each family have to be similarly marked to establish ownership. The Vintners' birds have two nicks cut in their beaks, those of the Dyers have one. These markings have almost certainly given rise to the well-known inn sign, the Swan with Two Necks, the last words in the name being a corruption of Nicks. Sometimes it occurs that the cygnets are of mixed parentage, cob and pen

Civic Customs

belonging to different owners, and in that case the brood is divided, half being marked like the father, and half like the mother. But if the numbers are uneven, then the last cygnet is given the cob's marking. The Queen's swans are not marked, for all unmarked swans are hers by right, but they are examined by the Uppers along with all the rest.

One of the oldest military ceremonies in Europe is the Ceremony of Her Majesty's Keys, which takes place every night in the Tower of London. This is the locking of the gates of the fortress against all enemies during the hours of darkness, and the handing-over of the Keys to the Resident Governor. At seven minutes to ten at night, the Chief Warder, in his long scarlet coat and Tudor bonnet, and carrying a candle-lantern and the keys of the different gates, comes from the Byward Tower and goes to the Bloody Tower Archway. There he is met by the Escort to the Keys, which consists of four guardsmen and a sergeant. He hands the lantern to the Drummer, or Bugler, of the Escort, and joins the ranks. All then march down Water Lane to the Byward Tower Archway, where they pick up the Watchman, also scarlet-coated, who goes with them as far as the Middle Tower, and there falls out in order to prepare the heavy gates for locking. The party goes on to the West Gate which the Chief Warder locks by the light of the lantern held by the Drummer, and the Escort present arms. The same ceremony takes place at the Middle and Byward Tower gates.

All then proceed again to the Bloody Tower Archway, where the sentry on duty challenges them with the words, ' Halt! Who comes there?' The Chief Warder says ' The Keys ', and the sentry asks ' Whose keys?' ' Queen Elizabeth's Keys ', replies the Chief Warder, and the sentry says, ' Advance, Queen Elizabeth's Keys. All's Well.' Thereupon the party does advance, goes through the Archway, and forms up facing the Main Guard. The Guard and the Escort present arms, and the Chief Warder, taking two paces forward, doffs his Tudor bonnet (which was a tin hat during the war) and cries ' God Preserve Queen Elizabeth!' Everyone answers ' Amen!' In spite of the ground covered, and the locking of the gates, all this has taken only seven minutes, and as the clock strikes ten, the Bugler sounds the Last Post. The Chief Warder then takes the Keys to the Queen's House, and leaves them in the care of the Resident Governor.

In the fourteenth century, Sir Robert Knollys (or Knolles)

and his wife, Constance, were granted a licence by the Corporation of London for the building of a hautpas, or high gallery, between two of Sir Robert's houses, which stood opposite each other in Seething Lane. For this privilege, they were required to render one red rose at Midsummer. Here we have a straightforward quit-rent in the form of a rose, of a type found in several others parts of England. This payment was punctually made for a long time, and then ceased, at some uncertain date, probably because the houses concerned had been demolished. But in 1924, the ceremony of rendering the rose to the City was revived by the Reverend T. B. Clayton, then Vicar of All-Hallows-by-the-Tower, Barking, and continued every Midsummer Day since then.

A curious legend has, however, grown up about the original transaction. It is now commonly believed that the rose was a penalty, not a rent, and that it was inflicted upon Sir Robert because he had built his hautpas without having obtained permission to do so. Another version of this tale adds that the fine was fixed simply as a rose, which would be very easy to produce in June, because Sir Robert, who was a notable soldier, had already performed great deeds for his country in war, and the corporation wished to show its gratitude thus. There is no evidence for either version of this tradition, and the records of the corporation do not support it. In fact, there seems to be little historic justification for the revival of a custom which probably died out several centuries ago. But however that may be, a fresh-plucked red rose, resting on a velvet cushion, is annually taken to the Mansion House on Midsummer Day by the churchwardens of All-Hallows-by-the-Tower, and is there ceremonially presented to the Lord Mayor by them, or sometimes, by some distinguished person of their choice.

One of the highlights of London's year is the Lord Mayor's Show, which now takes place on the second Saturday in November, though formerly on 9 November. The Lord Mayor is elected with great ceremony on 29 September, Michaelmas Day, but he does not actually begin his term of office until he has taken the customary oath on the appointed day in November. In the reign of King John it was laid down that the new Mayor (not known then as the Lord Mayor) must present himself for that purpose before the King himself, or in the latter's absence, before the Lord Chief Justice at the Law Courts. In practice, it has been the Lord Chief Justice, rather than the monarch, who has received the oath for many centuries. Originally the Lord Mayor travelled on horseback, or in the State barge, but since 1712, he has gone by coach. His present magnificent coach, gilded like something out of a fairy tale, was built in 1757. It is of immense size, and is drawn by six splendid shire horses whose normal everyday work is to draw the great drays of a well-known brewery company. From very early times, this colourful mayoral procession has been made an occasion for historical pageants and fine displays, which vary in their theme according to the special interests of the period. The first printed account of the show appeared in 1585, but the procession itself was by then more than 300 years old.

The City of London and its Lord Mayor enjoy certain rights and privileges which are not found in other towns of the kingdom. One is that the City Sword and the ward maces are carried upright in State processions, instead of being sloped over the shoulder of the bearer, as elsewhere. Another of a different kind, is that the Lord Mayor and some other City officials receive twice a year a gift of deer from the royal forests, a gift first bestowed upon their predecessors in 1428, when Sir Richard Whittington, of cat fame, held the mayoralty. The Queen and the Lord Mayor are the only two people outside the precincts of the Tower of London who know the password of that fortress by night. No troops may cross the City boundaries without his permision, nor, on the accession of a new monarch, may the Heralds enter to proclaim him or her without similar permission. Only certain regiments are allowed to march through the City streets with bayonets fixed, drums beating, and colours flying. These are the Blues and Royals, the Royal Fusiliers, the Royal Marines, the Queen's Regiment, the Grenadier Guards and the Coldstream Guards, all of which have some special past association with London on which their claim to this privilege is based. The Lord Mayor takes precedence over everyone in his City, and even the Queen has to ask leave of entry on ceremonial occasions. She is met on the site of old Temple Bar by the Lord Mayor, who surrenders his authority for so long as she remains in the City by offering her the hilt of the Pearl Sword. She touches, and returns it, and only then passes inwards, with the Lord Mayor and his company riding in procession before her.

One of the most interesting of our ancient customs is the Tynwald ceremony in the Isle of Man, which takes place on 5 July, Old Midsummer Day. On this annual occasion, the laws enacted by the Tynwald, or Manx Parliament, during the previous 12 months are read aloud, in Manx and in English, before the assembled people, and are then ratified by them. At one time, each separate measure was read in full, in both languages, but since 1865 only the titles and abstracts are given out. The reading and the ratification on this day are both essential, for no new law has any legal force in the island until this has been done.

The ceremony is held on Tynwald Hill, an artificial hill on an open space by St John's, which is traditionally said to have been built of earth brought from all the 17 parishes of the island. It is 12ft high, and has four circular platforms round it. Its name is derived from the Norse *Thing-vellir*, a place where the Thing, or open-air public assembly, was held. This was a democratic gathering well-known in Scandinavia during the Viking Age, at which new laws were introduced, disputes settled, and criminal cases heard and judged. It took place, usually, on some wide open space, where there was ample room for the many people who came to it from all over the district to build themselves temporary dwellings where they could live in comparative comfort during its duration. Usually also, there was a hill or eminence nearby on which the laws and the judgements arrived at could be proclaimed for all to hear. The people of Man, once overrun by Norsemen in the ninth and tenth centuries, would certainly have been familiar with this form of assembly, and with some changes, they have preserved it in modern form down to the present time.

Today, the ceremonies begin with a service in St John's Church, followed by a procession to the Tynwald Hill over a path strewn with rushes, as is the hill itself. These rushes were long supplied by the farmer of Ballaleece, who held his land by right of performing this annual service. The Lieutenant-Governor, representing the Queen, is preceded in the procession by the Sword-bearer, who carries the thirteenth-century Sword of State point upwards before him. On arrival at the hill, he mounts to the highest platform, and sits on a red velvet chair, facing eastwards, as tradition demands. Next to him sits the Bishop of Sodor and Man, the last of the island barons, and round them both stand the two Deemsters and the members of the Council. On the platform below, the 24 elected members of the House of Keys are assembled, and on the third terrace, the clergy, members of the Bar, and the High Bailiffs. The fourth, and lowest, platform holds minor officials of various kinds. The people of the island, whose consenting voices the rest of the company have really come to hear, stand on the grass all round the hill.

When all the company are assembled, the Coroner of Glen-faba rises to 'Fence the Court'. This is to protect it from all disturbances, brawls and quarrels for as long as it sits, and the Coroner does so by charging all present to abstain from any form of trouble-making, upon 'pain of death'. He then declares three times that the Court is fenced, and the business of the day begins. New Coroners are sworn in, and the abstracts and titles of the various new laws read, in English by the First Deemster, and in Manx by the Senior Coroner. The people then signify their consent by giving three cheers for the Queen. After this, the procession re-forms and returns to the church where the Lieut-enant-Governor signs the bills, and the Tynwald ceremonies end until Old Midsummer Day comes round again.

# 9 The Land and Its Customs

MANY ANCIENT CUSTOMS concerning the inheritance and tenancy of land still survive today, in spite of constant changes in the law during the passage of centuries, and the shifting of political ideas or economic conditions. Courts Leet and Courts Baron still function in a number of places. These courts have come down to us from the Middle Ages, and are still competent to regulate a variety of matters connected with the running of the manors to which they belong. Courts Leet, which are said to date from the time of Alfred the Great, are courts of record, which also have the power to enquire into cases of felony; Courts Baron deal chiefly with manorial rights, rents, and, tenures.

In the New Forest, there is a Court of Swainmote, better known as the Verderers' Court, which meets at Lyndhurst about six times a year. Its full title is the Court of Swainmote and

Attachment of the New Forest, and its function is to deal with matters of pasturage, the collection and sale of firewood, strayed or injured animals, pannage and turbary, and all similar matters. Pannage concerns the right of the commoners' pigs to browse on fallen acorns or beech-mast. Turbary is the right to take so many turves, a right which, in the New Forest, is attached to certain chimneys or hearths. It does not belong to any man, but to his chimney, and consequently all the commoners are very reluctant to alter their ancient chimneys or fireplaces, even if the cottage has otherwise been completely modernized. If they do so, their turbary privileges are forfeited. There is another Verderers' Court in the Forest of Dean, which meets at regular intervals in the Speech House, in the depths of the Forest. This court is less busy than that at Lyndhurst, partly because there are not so many animals to protect and deal with as there are in the New Forest, but it still retains many of its old powers, and works alongside the Forestry Commission to preserve the amenities of the Forest.

In Derbyshire, the rights and privileges of the lead-miners are controlled by the Great Barmote Courts, which are said to be the oldest industrial courts in this country. They were brought into being by Edward I at the Inquisition of Ashbourne in 1288, one for the High Peak at Monyash (but afterwards transferred to Ashford-in-the-Water), and one at Wirksworth for the Low Peak. The lead-mining industry has very greatly declined during recent years, but its affairs are still earnestly discussed, two or three times a year, by the Barmote Courts, as of old.

The centuries-old Court Leet of the Savoy Liberty, in London, meets regularly to deal with any matters affecting the safety and order of its buildings, and the welfare of the inhabitants. It can inflict fines for disorderly conduct within the boundaries of the Liberty, or for the neglect of houses or other buildings, and it can deal rigorously with undesirable residents. The amount of the fines is fixed by the jury, and the money so obtained is used for the support of the Court.

A less ancient, but nevertheless quite long-established court is the Admiralty Court of the City of Rochester, which meets annually, in early July, in a decorated barge in the river Medway. It was set up in 1729 by Act of Parliament ' for Regulating, well-ordering, Governing and Improving the Oyster Fishery in the River Medway and waters thereof ', and its sole business today is the administration of the oyster fisheries in the river. In its present form, it consists of the aldermen of the city, and a fishery jury made up of freemen of the river, presided over by the Mayor of Rochester who, since the fifteenth century, has also been known as Admiral of the Medway.

A very odd manorial custom connected with the Honour of Rayleigh, in Essex, existed at Rochford, in the same county, until well towards the end of last century. This was the meeting at cockcrow on the Wednesday following Michaelmas Day, of what was known as the Great Lawless Court. Originally, it met at Rayleigh, but was later transferred to Rochford, where it met in a field called King's Hill, so named, according to tradition, after the earlier meeting-place at Rayleigh. In this field there was a white-painted post, and round this the business of this strange court was conducted.

Through the darkness of the early October morning, Steward and tenants came to the post without the help of lighted lanterns, for they were not allow to carry them. What light was absolutely necessary for the work of the court was provided by a man bearing a single torch. The Steward called the names of the tenants in a whisper, and in the same way they answered. Their rents and other dues were paid in almost complete silence. No one was allowed to speak to anyone else, except under his breath. ' They are all to whisper to each other ', remarks Philip Morant, in his *History and Antiquities of the County of Essex* (1768), ' nor have they any pen and ink, but supply that office with a coal.' Anyone who failed to attend this extraordinary meeting, when summoned, was liable to be severely fined.

A similar meeting, called the Little Lawless Court, used to be held in the same place on Hock Monday, but this seems to have disappeared fairly early, leaving only the Great Lawless Court at Michaelmas. However, the two at Rochford were not the only examples of this type of gathering in Essex. At one time, there was another at Epping, which met under a maple tree that grew between the church and Eppingbury. Though no one really knows the origin of these three courts, it has been suggested that they began, far off in time, as primitive community meetings held under, or round, some guardian tree; and also, that the white post in the Rochford field, and the earlier one at Rayleigh from which it was copied, sprang from a vague folk memory of such a tree. For the darkness and the silence, no very

I

clear explanation seems to be forthcoming, though a rather improbable legend of medieval tenants conspiring against their lord has sometimes been told to account for the Rochford Court.

In its last years, towards the end of the nineteenth century, the Great Lawless Court degenerated into a sort of revel, with a good deal of cock-crowing and the flourishing of forbidden lanterns, and a general tendency to treat the whole thing as a joke. In consequence, it gradually fell into desuetude, and is now heard of no more. There is, however, no doubt that, in its long heyday, it was a completely serious gathering, as indeed, the heavy fines imposed upon the tenants for non-attendance are quite enough to show.

Another curious ' lawless ' custom may be mentioned here, though it is not a manorial matter, but a popular jollification. This was the Lawless Hour, known as Kellums, which formerly took place at Kidderminster on Michaelmas Day. On that day, a new bailiff was elected, and between the beginning of his term of office, and the end of that of his predecessor, there was a pause, during which the borough was virtually without government. The townspeople took full advantage of it. As soon as the town bell was sounded at three o'clock, the streets filled with jovial crowds, all merrily engaged in throwing cabbage-stalks at each other. In due course, the bailiff-elect went to pay a ceremonial visit to his predecessor, accompanied by the other civic officers and a drum-and-fife band. An unruly mob of townsmen ran alongside the procession and pelted the bailiff and all his companions with apples. Practically everybody seems to have taken part in this diversion including, according to a contributor to the *Gentleman's Magazine* for 1790, ' the most respectable families in the town '. He adds, ' I have known forty pots of apples expended at one house '. While the Lawless Hour lasted, no one could be arrested for damage to property, and only in extreme cases for personal injuries. It is frequently said that this singular custom was suppressed at the end of the eighteenth century, but according to another account, it was not finally swept away until about 1845.

Of ancient quit-rents still surviving, two of the most interesting are those rendered in London every October for two properties, one at Eardington in Shropshire, and the other a forge, long since vanished, in St Clement Danes' parish. Both are known to have existed as far back as the thirteenth century, and both are now rendered by the City Solicitor in the Royal Courts of Justice on a day between Michaelmas and Martinmas.

The ceremony begins with the service due for the land known as The Moors, at Eardington. The Queen's Remembrancer calls upon 'the tenants and occupiers of a piece of waste land called The Moors, in the County of Salop' to 'come forth and do your service'. The City Solicitor, representing the Corporation of London, then chops a small faggot of wood with a hatchet and another with a billhook, and presents these implements to the Queen's Remembrancer who acknowledges the cutting of the faggots with the words 'Good Service'. Originally, instead of the hatchet and billhook, two knives had to be presented, one sharp enough to cut in half with a single blow a hazel stick of one year's growth, the other too 'weak' to make any serious mark upon it. At some unrecorded date, these two knives were superseded by the hatchet and billhook of today.

The Forge has then to be paid for by the presentation of six very large horseshoes, each pierced for ten nails, and 61 nails of appropriate size. The Queen's Remembrancer receives them, and says 'Good Number'. The horseshoes and nails, which are all of great age, are kept in the office of the Queen's Remembrancer during the year, and are returned to the City officials in time for the October ceremony. The hatchet and billhook, on the other hand, are new for each occasion.

The interesting thing about the Forge is that it no longer exists, and has not done so for a very long time, but the horseshoes and nails continued to be given for it regularly all the same. Its exact site was unknown for many years, but entries newly found in the City documents indicate that it was somewhere near where Australia House now stands. It is recorded in the Great Roll of the Exchequer for 1235 that a piece of land in St Clement Dane's parish was granted to Walter le Brun, a farrier, on which to build a forge. For this, he paid a quit-rent of six horseshoes and 61 nails. In the Patent Rolls, 1258–60, there is an entry concerning a further grant of land to Walter le Mareschall (or Farrier), who may have been the same man, or his son, comprising a triangular piece of ground called the Gore, now partly covered by Australia House.

Many other lands are still held by the performance of some service, or by the presentation of some object such as a rose, or gloves, or some pepper, or a salmon spear, on a particular occcasion. These services, or dues, may lapse for years because they are not demanded, but unless they are legally abolished, they continue to exist and may be revived at any time. The Dukes of Wellington and Marlborough both render a flag for the great mansions presented to them by a grateful nation. On the anniversary of the Battle of Waterloo, 18 June, the Duke of Wellington hangs a new tricolour flag above the bust of his great ancestor in the Guard Room at Windsor Castle as quit-rent for Stratfieldsaye; and on 2 August, anniversary of the Battle of Blenheim, the Duke of Marlborough presents another flag, the golden Fleur-de-Lys on a white ground, as payment for Blenheim Palace. This also hangs in the Guard Room at Windsor, over the bust of the first Duke of Marlborough. The Ailesbury family hold Savernake Forest by the service of blowing a horn when the monarch comes to visit the estate. The Downes of Taxal were required to blow a horn on Midsummer Day, ' standing on the heights of Windgather ', and also to hold the King's stirrup whenever he came to hunt in Macclesfield Forest. The Lord of Hoton also had to hold his stirrup when he mounted his horse at the castle in Carlisle. Wyfold Court in Oxfordshire was held by the presentation of a red rose whenever the sovereign passed that way on May morning, a tenure service perhaps a little more difficult to fulfil than some of the others since the calendar change of 1752 made roses in bloom on 1 May less plentiful than they once were.

Wroth Silver is still paid before sunrise, as it is said to have been paid, with only a few breaks, for a thousand years. On the morning of St Martin's Day (11 November), representatives of the 25 parishes of Knightlow Hundred come very early to Knightlow Hill, to pay their dues to the Duke of Buccleuch, who is Lord of the Hundred. They gather round all that is now left of Knightlow Cross, and listen while the Duke's agent reads the Charter of Assembly. Then each person in turn steps forward, as the agent calls upon him, and drops the money due from his parish into a hollow in a great stone that was once the base of the vanished Cross. As he does so, he says ' Wroth Silver '; at one time he was required also to walk three times round the stone before he deposited his money in the hollow. When all the payments have been made, the whole company repair to the Dun Cow Inn at Dunchurch, where they toast the

Duke in rum and milk, and are given breakfast at his expense.

This custom is supposed to be of Anglo-Saxon origin, and to represent an ancient payment for the right to drive cattle over Dunsmore Heath or, according to another tradition, for exemption from military service. Originally such payments were made to the sovereign, but the privilege of receiving Wroth Silver was bestowed by Charles I upon the Duke of Buccleuch, in whose family it has since remained. The amounts due are very small, the total sum adding up to no more than 9s 4d (a little over 46p), which can hardly cover the cost of breakfast for all at the Dun Cow. Payment is nevertheless rigidly enforced, as is the hour at which it must be made. Defaulters are required to pay 20s for every penny left unpaid, or alternatively, a white bull with red ears and a red nose. The latter, which sounds like one of the old wild cattle of England, now practically extinct, would surely be almost impossible to find today, though it is said (*Notes and Queries*, 16 December 1893) that such a fine was imposed on a defaulter during the nineteenth century.

The people of Wishford Magna in Wiltshire maintain their right to gather wood in the nearby Grovely Forest by the observance of an ancient custom which now takes place on 29 May, though actually it has nothing to do with the Restoration. The wood-gathering privileges preserved by this custom are, in fact, much older than that royal event, and are described in a document dated 1603, and known as the Book of Rights. This is a record of the proceedings of a court held in the forest on 15 May 1603 wherein ' the olde auntient and laudable customes ' of Great Wishford and its neighbour, Barford St Martin, are clearly set forth and signed by a number of local men, one of whom has the curious and distinctive name of Catkat. Of the privileges mentioned in this record, some have now been lost, or commuted for money payments, but the right to gather ' deade snappinge Boughes and Stickes ' at any time, and once a year, ' one loade of trees upon a Cart to be drawen by strength of peopell ' still remains. But public claim must annually be made for it, and it is this claim which is now made every year on 29 May. Originally it was made on Whit Tuesday, and was perhaps shifted to Oak Apple Day, when that festival was still young, as a sign of loyalty.

Before sunrise, the young men of the parish march through the village street with drums and bugles and other noise-making instruments, and waking everyone as they go with shouts of 'Grovely! Grovely! And All Grovely!' The villagers thus roused from slumber look out of their windows and greet them, and then the cheerful band goes on into Grovely Forest to gather green branches wherewith to decorate their houses, and to be carried in the processions held later in the day. One large branch, decorated with ribbons and known as the Marriage Bough, is hauled up to the top of the church tower, and left there to bring luck to all who are married in the church during the following year. All these branches have to be ' drawen by strength of people ' as the Book of Rights says, not by horse-drawn carts and still less, of course, my motor vehicles. Handcarts are allowed, and so are bicycles. When these first became fashionable, their use was carefully debated, and finally permitted, since they too needed human strength to move them.

Since 1951, the old custom of going to Salisbury to claim the forest rights has been revived. In the 1603 Book of Rights, it is stated that ' the lords, freeholders, Tennants and Inhabitance of the Mannor of greate Wishford . . . have used to goe in a daunce to the Cathedral Church of our blessed Ladie in the Citte of newe Sarum on Whit Tuesdaie in the said Countie of Wiltes, and their made theire clayme to theire custome in the Forrest of Grovley in theis words; Groveley Groveley and all Groveley.' This custom, which was already very old in 1603, seems to have persisted down to the early nineteenth century, and then ceased because a kind of unofficial fair, with stalls and booths, had developed round it on the green, and the cathedral authorities objected. The dance and the shouted claim thereafter took place at Wishford Rectory, though for some years two women continued to go into Salisbury and reverently lay oak boughs on the high altar of the great church. But in 1951, old ways were restored, and the ancient claim is once more publicly made inside the cathedral, and a dance performed outside on the green.

The four women who dance also walk in the procession which follows their return from the city, carrying small faggots on their heads. This procession starts from the Town-End Tree, at the south end of the village, and includes the May Queen and her attendants, men and women in fancy dress, and members of the Oak Apple Club carrying oak boughs and a banner. This club was founded in 1892 to preserve the rights and privileges of the parish, as laid down in the Book of Rights. Only genuine residents of Great Wishford are entitled to belong to it. Hand-carts of the type used to gather wood, now gaily decorated, also appear in the procession. Afterwards there is a ceremonial lunch, Maypole dancing, a fête, and other amusements lasting the rest of the day.

In the procession, a sieve containing seven dolls is sometimes carried. This commemorates a persistent local legend concerning the seven children said to have been born at one birth, to Edith Bonham in the fifteenth century. Tradition says that she first had twins, and her husband, Thomas Bonham, being, as Aubrey remarks in his *Natural History of Wiltshire*, 'troubled at it', departed on his travels, and was absent for seven years, during which time he neither communicated with his wife, nor cut his hair or his nails. But being warned by a witch that Edith had given him up for dead and intended to marry again, he hastened home, only to find that she did not recognize him, which, after seven years, was perhaps not altogether surprising. However, he was able to produce one half of a ring he had broken with her before he left, and so convinced her that he was indeed her husband. A year later, she gave birth to seven children, who are supposed to have been taken to church for baptism in a large sieve. Thomas Bonham was Lord of the Manor of Wishford, and he and his wife are both buried in Wishford Church. On their monument there were once nine brass effigies of children, six of which have now disappeared, though the marks made by them upon the stone are still clearly visible.

Probably these nine brasses simply represent the number of children born to the Bonhams during the course of their married life, but the legend of the seven born at one time is very persistent. It occurs in other places as well, the number of children being usually seven, and always agreeing with the number of years the husband is absent. It is told at Upton Scudamore, also in Wiltshire, and at Chumleigh, in Devon. In the latter place, a poor man was the father of seven children, and he was so horrified at the prospect of having to feed and raise so many at once that he determined to drown them all. He put them in a sack and set out, but on his way to the nearest convenient water, he encountered the Countess of Devon, who at once asked him what he had in the sack. He replied 'Puppies', but evidently she did not believe him, for she insisted on the sack being opened. When she saw the children, she took them away and placed them in the care of the Church, founding seven prebends for their support. These prebends were afterwards consolidated with the rectory.

The celebrated trial for the Dunmow Flitch, which still takes place on Whit Monday (or the Spring Holiday) at Great Dunmow, Ilford, or Saffron Walden, has now become more of a joke than anything else, but it has a long and respectable history, running back for at least 600 years, and probably longer. We hear first of the flitch being awarded in 1445, when Richard Wright, of Bawburgh, won it, but the custom seems to have been well known long before that date, for both William Langland and Chaucer mention it, casually and without explanation, as though their readers would certainly be familiar with it. Philip Morant, the Essex historian, suggests in *The History & Antiquities of the County of Essex* (1768) that it may have started in Saxon or Norman times as a manorial obligation, ' a burthen upon the estate as the same custom was at Wichener in Staffordshire'. It is usually said to have been instituted in the thirteenth century by one of the Fitzwalter family, but of this there is no definite proof.

In its original form, any man who had been married for at least a year and a day, or any longer period, and during that time had never regretted his marriage, nor wished himself single again, could go to Little Dunmow Priory, and lay his claim for a flitch of bacon. He had to make his sworn statement while kneeling on two sharp stones in the presence of the Prior, the monks and an assembly of local people. If his claim was allowed, he received the bacon, and was carried triumphantly in procession, seated in the Prior's chair. This old, narrow, and very uncomfortable wooden seat is kept in Little Dunmow Church now, and modern winners of the flitch are carried in something newer and more capacious. After Richard Wright, Stephen Samuel of Little Easton, is recorded as a winner in 1467, and in 1510, Thomas, the fuller of Coggeshall. There was then a prolonged pause. The next award was not made until 1701.

At a Court Baron presided over by the Steward of Little Dunmow Manor, John and Anne Reynolds, and also William and Jane Parsley, received a gammon of bacon for each pair. This was a memorable trial for two reasons. One was that, for the first time, the wives were definitely included in the award. Hitherto they had not been mentioned, and what they thought about their husbands' claims is unknown. The other was that, also for the first time, there was a jury, consisting in this case of five young women. By 1751, this jury had grown to six bachelors and six spinsters, which it still is. This was the last of the true manorial awards, the successful candidates on this occasion being Thomas and Ann Shakespeare. Thereafter we hear of various lords of the manor refusing to continue the old custom. Certain keen individuals organized private awards of their own, but after 1751 the Flitch custom may be said to have died out until 1855. Then, mainly through the enthusiasm of William Harrison Ainsworth, author of *The Flitch of Bacon*, it was revived, though at Great, not Little Dunmow. Ainsworth himself presented two flitches, which were won by a couple named Barlow, and another named de Chatelain. From then on, there were other celebrations of the same kind, and now the ' trial ' has become an annual event. It has, of course, no longer any manorial meaning. A ' judge ' has replaced the old Steward of the Manor; everything is done in imitation of a real, but comic law court, and the applicant has to be prepared to face a searching cross-examination, as well as a great deal of hilarity from the spectators. For most people, it is a cheerful, rollicking affair, but sometimes serious claims are made, as of old, and for such sincere claimants there is usually a special flitch given.

Land and grazing rights are sometimes let for short periods by auctions of peculiar forms. In the seventeenth and eighteenth centuries, candle auctions were very common, and some still survive today. At Aldermaston, in Berkshire, a meadow known as Church Acre is auctioned every three years at Easter. The land belongs to the parish church, and the rents are used for church expenses. A lighted candle is provided, into which a pin is thrust, about an inch below the flame. Bidding goes on until the pin falls out, the last man to make a bid before it does so becoming the holder of the meadow for the next three years. At Tatworth, in Somerset, a piece of ground called Stowell Mead, which includes a watercress bed, is let for a year at a time by candle auction held on the Tuesday following 6 April, Old Lady Day. Here there is no pin, but the last bid before the candle burns out wins Stowell Mead.

At Chedzoy, in the same county, there is another Church Acre which is auctioned by candle every 21 years, and is said to have been so regularly since the fifteenth century. It claims to be the oldest candle auction in the country, and very probably it is. Collinson tells us, in his *History of the County of Somerset* (1791), of a very interesting custom that formerly took place at Congresbury on the Saturday before Old Midsummer Day. Two pieces of common land, the East and West Dolemoors, were divided into acres, each acre being clearly marked with a distinctive mark cut upon the turf. A number of apples were then marked in the same way, put into a bag, and distributed to each of the commoners present. The plots of land were then claimed according to the mark on the apple received. Four other acres were then auctioned by inch of candle, and the money put to pay for the apple distribution and a subsequent meal.

At Wishford Magna there is an auction of another kind which is known as the sale of the Midsummer Tithes. The grazing rights of two pieces of water meadow are let by the parish church, upon which some unknown donor bestowed them at some now forgotten date, from Rogation Monday until Old Lammas Day (12 August), not by a candle but by the setting of the sun. On the evening of Rogation Monday, the parish clerk, or someone nominated by him, goes to the church and begins to walk up and down between the porch and the churchyard gate, with the door key in his hand. While he does so, those present make their bids. This goes on for so long as the sun remains above the horizon, but the moment it disappears from sight, the clerk strikes the gate with his key. The man whose bid was the last made before the gate was struck acquires the grazing rights until the end of the season.

Bourne in Lincolnshire has an auction at Easter which depends on the energies of young lads. In 1770, a local man named Richard Clay made provision in his will for an annual gift of bread to be made to the poor of Eastgate Ward. To pay for this, he left a piece of ground, now known as White Bread Meadow, which was to be auctioned every year at Easter, as it still is. While it lasts, two boys run up and down a defined length of road, and bids are made for so long as they are moving. The auction ends only when no bid has been received during the double run to the fixed point on the road and back again to the starting place. The successful bidder then becomes the lessee of the White Bread Meadow for the following year. The boys are rewarded for their running, and then all who took part in the auction share a supper of bread and cheese, spring onions, and beer.

A centuries-old method of apportioning strips of grassland is still used at Yarnton in Oxfordshire. Two meadows, known as West Mead and Pixey Mead, are divided into strips of varying size, and once a year, lots are drawn for them by the free-holders of Yarnton, Wolvercote and Begbroke, who own the mowing rights. Until fairly recently, there was a third meadow – Oxhay – which was thus divided, but when the Witney by-pass was built most of this meadow passed into the hands of the road-makers, and cannot now be included in the lot-drawing.

In July, when the hay is ready for cutting, the Head Meads-man fixes a day, and the lessees of the mowing rights, or those to whom they have sold their hay in advance, go down to the meadows. All the strips are marked out by stakes, with the exception of the Tydals, which are portions permanently assigned to the rectories of Yarnton and Begbroke in lieu of tithes, and are not affected by the lot-drawing. The Head Meadsman carries a bag in which are 13 wooden balls, known as Mead Balls. They are very old, and each one has a name upon it – Gilbert, Harry, White, Boat, William, Rothe, Walter, Jeoffrey, Freeman, Green, Dunn, Perry, Boulton, and Watery Molly. Who first bore these names long ago is not known now, but what the balls mean today is quite clear. Each one represents a certain acreage, or a specified quantity of the total acreage, which falls to a man's share when he draws it from the bag. The situation of the land corresponding with these names varies from year to year, so as to give every man in turn a chance of the better as well as the poorer parts of the meadows.

The lot-drawing begins about eight o'clock in the morning. When a ball is drawn, some of the grass is cut with a few sweeps of the scythe, and the initials of the man to whom the strip has fallen are cut upon the ground. Formerly, it was usual for a number of men to ' run the treads ', or mark the boundaries between one strip and another, by running fast up and down them shuffling their feet as they went, but this part of the work is now done by tractors. When the lot-drawing is quite finished, mowing begins at once.

The Lot Meadow Mowing was made the occasion for a sort of festival until the beginning of the last century. There was a mowing feast, and an unofficial ' fair '; there was also a Garland which was raced for and, when won, hung in the church until the next Lot Meadow Mowing came round. It was customary for each meadow to be mowed in a single day, which usually meant bringing in a number of labourers from outside the village. In due course, the ' fair ' and the other festivities attracted idlers and others, and the gathering became disorderly and rowdy. Fights and disturbances were common. In 1817, there was a riot, during which a man was killed. From then on, it was arranged that three days should be allowed for each meadow, thereby doing away with the need for importing strangers from elsewhere. This change did away with the various forms of rowdiness, and eventually, the holiday character of the assembly altered also. The ' fair ' and the feast and the Garland all slowly died away; and today the Lot Meadow Mowing, though it is a cherished custom of the parish, is simply a sober and straightforward farming custom, like any other.

# 10 Memories

ON THE LAST SUNDAY IN AUGUST, which is Wakes Sunday in Eyam, the people of that Derbyshire village remember their own heroic past. In 1665, when the plague was raging in London, the local tailor received, during Wakes Week, a box of cloth which had been sent to him from the capital. This cloth was infected, and within a month every one in the tailor's house, except the man himself was dead of the plague. Moreover, the disease was spreading through the other houses of the parish with terrifying speed. It soon became clear that little could be done for the unfortunate place itself, but the rector, William Mompesson, realized that the infection might yet be stopped from spreading to the surrounding districts if his people would agree not to fly from the danger, but instead to remain, voluntarily, in their homes until the epidemic was over. With the help of Thomas Stanley, his Nonconformist predecessor who had been ejected from the living after the Restoration, but still lived in Eyam, he did persuade the parishioners to take this heroic course, and the promise, once given, was kept by all until the end.

It is, perhaps, one thing to make a promise to stay on the spur of the moment, and something rather different to keep it during 13 weary months, with one's friends and relatives dying one by one all round. But it was this which the people of Eyam had to do, and which they did. No one was allowed to enter the village, and no one could go more than half a mile from it. The Earl of Devonshire supplied them all with food and other necessities, which he caused to be left by a certain stone, far enough away to be safe for those he sent, and near enough for the Eyam men who were still well enough to go and fetch it. The church was closed, but an open-air service was held every Sunday in a large hollow called Cucklet Dell, where the Rector preached to his people from a rock. The plague abated somewhat during the winter, but it broke out again as fiercely as ever in the following May. When it ended in October 1666, 259 people had died out of a total population of 350, amongst them Catherine Mompesson, the Rector's wife.

The sacrifice made by the villagers was not wasted. The infection was held, and except for a few cases of plague in the hamlet of Foolow, about two miles off (said to have been carried by an Eyam dog), in the first October of the epidemic, no one outside suffered. Now, on Wakes Sunday, there is a memorial service for the parishioners who died. A long procession headed by a band and led by Anglican and Nonconformist clergy, goes out to Cucklet Dell, where a service is held and a sermon preached, as of old, and a special hymn called the ' Plague Hymn ' is sung.

A medieval victory, which is, rather oddly, commemorated annually on the wrong day, is the Battle of Neville's Cross which was fought in 1346. When Edward III was away in France, the Scots under David I took the opportunity of invading England, and came as far south as Co. Durham before they were halted by Queen Phillipa's forces. On 17 October they were decisively defeated at a spot on the Red Hills, not far from Durham, where one of the Nevilles had, long before, set up a great stone cross.

On the night before the battle, John Fossor, Prior of Durham, had a dream (or perhaps a vision), in which he was bidden to go next day to a certain place near the cross, and to take with him as a banner, the sacred cloth which St Cuthbert had used to cover the chalice when he was saying Mass. This was one of the abbey's most treasured relics, and afterwards it became the battle standard of the men of Durham, which they carried at Flodden Field and during the Pilgrimage of Grace. The Prior took it to the battlefield, as he had been told, and all that day, he and the monks who had come with him stood round it and prayed for victory, while the battle raged on. In the meantime, the rest of the abbey monks congregated on the tower to pray for the Queen's army and their Prior's safety, and to see what they could of the distant fight; and when at last, victory became certain, it was their joyous *Te Deum* that first conveyed the good news to the townspeople.

Afterwards, thanksgiving for the country's deliverance was annually offered on the tower, at first by the monks until the dissolution of the monasteries dispersed them, and then by the choristers of Durham Cathedral. The date of this ceremony was, naturally, 17 October, the anniversary of the battle, but in the seventeenth century it was altered to 29 May, probably as part of the general expression of loyalty to the returned King Charles II. But 29 May or not, every Durham man knows that this ceremony has nothing really to do with Charles, and is only concerned with a north-country victory of the fourteenth century.

At the end of Evensong, the choir ascend the central tower and sing anthems on three sides of it – the east, north and south – but not the west. Why the west is omitted, no one really knows, but there is a tradition to the effect that someone once fell from it, long ago, and was killed. This is usually said to have been a chorister, and perhaps it was, but the whole legend is very uncertain. There is another local legend concerned with the cross which gave its name to the battle. During the Reformation, Neville's Cross was destroyed, and only a stump was left. It is said that if any one walks nine times round the stump, and then puts his ear to the ground, he will hear cries and the clashing of arms, and all the noises of a medieval battle. But this, too, like the story of the chorister, is uncertain.

A battle much nearer to us in time is remembered on 1 August, sometimes called Minden Day, the anniversary of the day on which the Battle of Minden was fought and won in 1759. The men of six famous British regiments which took part in the battle – the Royal Hampshire Regiment, the Queen's Own

Scottish Borderers, the Queen's Own Yorkshire Light Infantry, the Lancashire Fusiliers, the Royal Welch Fusiliers, and the Suffolk Regiment (now amalgamated with the Royal Norfolk to form the 1st East Anglian Regiment) – all have the right to wear roses in their hats on this day, and to adorn their colours and drums with the same flower.

This is because, in 1759, these regiments were ordered to be ready to advance upon a large body of French cavalry on the far side of Minden Heath. Through a mistake, the men started off too soon, and alone. As they crossed the heath, they saw that the rose briars were in bloom, and lightheartedly plucked the flowers as they passed, thrusting them into their hats and into their equipment. So bedecked, they swept forward on their premature attack, which was successful, and both then and later in the day, played a great and gallant part in the total victory.

Trafalgar Day is 21 October, the anniversary of the Battle of Trafalgar in 1805, and of the death of Lord Nelson. In his later days, Nelson was the hero of the people, their strong protection against the French; in Devonshire, he was sometimes said to be a reincarnation of that other great hero, Sir Francis Drake. Countess Brownlow records in her *Slight Reminiscences of a Septuagenarian* (1867) that for most people the splendid news of the victory at Trafalgar was entirely overshadowed by the accompanying tiding of Nelson's death, and she goes on to remark that the coaches which carried the news into every part of the country bore black mourning ribbons over their victory evergreens. Now, on Trafalgar Day, Nelson's memory is honoured in London and in Portsmouth by special ceremonies. Wreaths are laid at the foot of his garlanded monument in Trafalgar Square. An anchor of laurel leaves comes every year from the descendants of the officers who fought at Trafalgar, and there are bunches of evergreens from the modern Navy ships which bear the same names as those which took part in the battle. At Portsmouth, the *Victory* is adorned with garlands, and Nelson's famous signal is flown by all the ships in the dockyard. A wreath is laid on *Victory*'s quarterdeck, where he was struck down, and a short religious service is held.

The celebrations held at Stratford-on-Avon on Shakespeare's birthday have long since grown from a local ceremony to an international event. The town is filled with visitors of every nationality, and the flags of many nations fly from tall, shield-bearing poles all down the centre of Bridge Street. Poets and ambassadors, actors, men of letters, delegates from British and foreign learned societies, tourists from afar, and ordinary people stream into Stratford to do homage to the man whose greatness is acknowledged all over the world, to visit his birthplace and his grave in the church, which is smothered with magnificent wreaths, simple posies, and masses of spring flowers of all sorts.

All this is very splendid, but for a few years, Oxford paid him a more homely homage on the same day. From 1938 onwards it was the custom for the mayor and representatives of the city and university to go with ceremony on 23 April from the town hall to the Painted Room in No. 3 Cornmarket, and there drink his health in sack and malmsey. The Painted Room, besides being very beautiful, has an interesting story of its own. In Tudor times, the house which contains it was the Crown Tavern, and was occupied by John Davenant, a freeman of the Merchant Taylors' Company in London, and later Mayor of Oxford. He was Shakespeare's friend, and father of his godson, William, who later became Sir William Davenant, the poet. In the Crown Tavern, Shakespeare used to stay on his way home to Stratford; ' Mr William Shakespeare ', says Aubrey, ' was wont to goe into Warwickshire once a yeare, and did commonly lye at this house in Oxon, where he was greatly respected.' It is very probable that at such times he slept in the Painted Room.

The existence of this room was unknown, or at least, long forgotten, until 1927, and was then discovered only by chance. The house was then occupied by a firm of tailors. Mr E. W. Attwood, needing more space for his workers, decided to turn one of the upper rooms into an extra workroom. Before he could do this, he was required by Board of Trade regulations to limewash the walls, which meant tearing down thick layers of old wallpaper and removing a Victorian fireplace in the east wall. Behind the latter, an old hearth was found, with the letters ' I.H.S.' above it, perhaps dating from the late fifteenth century when the property belonged to New College, and was used for New College students. But this unexpected find was only a beginning. On the north wall there was oak panelling of the year 1630, and under it a very fine example of mural painting dating from about 1550. On a rich red-orange ground-

K

work, there were compartments made by interlaced figures of old gold, outlined alternately in black and white. These covered most of the wall, leaving only space at the top for a running motto. Each compartment held posies of windflowers, Canterbury bells, passion flowers, wild roses and lilies, and bunches of grapes, all with their colours as bright and glowing as they had been when they were first painted. Along the top of the wall are the words:

> First of thy Rising And last of thi rest
> be thou gods servante for that I hold best
> In the mornynge earlye
> Serve god Devoutlye
> Fear god above allthynge
> and                and the Kynge.

The last two lines are on the east wall, which is also painted as far as the fireplace.

The Painted Room is on the second floor and, following the usual pattern of a tavern of the time, would have been the best guest-room. Here Shakespeare must have slept, and it must have been the mural paintings that he saw, and not the panelling, for the latter dates only from 1630, by which time he had been dead for 14 years. Mr Attwood, realizing at once the dangers that might face this lovely room with any change of tenancy, put it in the care of the Oxford Preservation Trust. The custom of ceremonially drinking to Shakespeare there on his birthday began in 1938 and continued for 30 years; but in 1968, the floor was pronounced unsafe, and the use of the room by more than 14 people at a time was forbidden. The Shakespeare gathering is, in fact, still held, from time to time, but in the nearby Golden Cross, not in its old home.

Lichfield honours Dr Johnson, who was born in that city, on 18 September (his birthday) with a ceremonial procession, and the laying of a wreath at the foot of his statue. The Cathedral choir recites his last prayer on the steps of his house, and sings hymns that were known in his time. On the same day, in Uttoxeter, there is another memorial of a different kind. Dr Johnson's father, Michael Johnson, had a stall in Uttoxeter market-place, and wanted his son to serve there with him, but he would not, and this caused a bitter and lasting quarrel between the two. The breach was still unhealed when Michael Johnson

died, and his son's genuine repentance came too late; but he
could, and did, make public penance for his share in the quarrel
by standing for several hours, bareheaded and in the pouring rain
at the place where his father had worked without his help. A
memorial plaque marks the spot now. On 18 September, the
schoolchildren gather in the market-place to hear the story of this
episode in a great man's life, and afterwards, one of them lays
a wreath by the memorial plaque. In the evening, the Johnson
Society usually holds a commemorative supper, lit by candles,
at which Dr Johnson's favourite dishes are traditionally served.

London remembers its great historian, John Stow, by a charming ceremony which was initiated in the early years of this
century, and has since been organized annually by the London
and Middlesex Archaeological Society. When Stow wrote his
famous *Survey of London* in 1598, he included in it a list of
all the City officials from the time of the Conquest down to his
own day. He died on 5 April 1605, and was buried in the church
of St Andrew Undershaft. His effigy there has a quill pen in its
hand, and writes forever in a large ledger. Now, on, or as near
as possible to, 5 April, the Lord Mayor of London, the Sheriffs,
and other City dignitaries attend a service in the church, and
then, standing before his monument, offer a prayer of thanksgiving for his life and work. The Lord Mayor then removes the
quill pen, and places another in the stone hand. The old pen
is given to the school in which one of the pupils has won the
John Stow essay contest for that year.

When Sir John Gayer died in 1649, he left direction in his
will that a sermon commemorating an incident in his career was
to be preached every year in the London church of St Katharine
Cree. This is the Lion Sermon, which is given every year on
16 October, unless that day falls on a Sunday, when the sermon
is moved to the nearest weekday. Sir John was a merchant who
became Lord Mayor of London in 1646 and again in 1647.
During the latter year, he was imprisoned for his firm refusal to
subsidize Parliament out of the City funds, a refusal which needed
both courage and determination in those troubled times. The
Lion Sermon commemorates an adventure which befell him on
one of his trading expeditions in the desert. Becoming separated
by some accident, from his companions, he was suddenly confronted by a lion. Being unarmed, there was nothing he could
do, except fall on his knees and pray for deliverance. His prayer

was answered; the lion looked at him, and went away. On his return to England, he gave in thanksgiving a number of charitable gifts and bequests, and made provision in his will for a memorial sermon on the anniversary of his miraculous escape.

On 21 May 1471, Henry VI died very suddenly in the Oratory of the Wakefield Tower, in the Tower of London, where he was then a prisoner. His Yorkist enemies said that he had perished of ' pure displeasure and melancholy ', but there is little doubt that he was murdered. Tradition has it that he was killed by Richard, Duke of Gloucester, who later became Richard III. He is said to have been struck down whilst praying in the Oratory. Now, on the anniversary of his death, he is remembered by Eton College and King's College, Cambridge, both of which he founded, in the memorial custom known as the Ceremony of the Lilies and Roses. Representatives of both these houses walk in procession with the Beefeaters and the Chaplain of the Tower to the Oratory, and there, about six o'clock in the evening, a service is held during which a prayer written by Henry himself is used. Then, on each side of the marble tablet in the floor which marks the place where the king fell, flowers are laid – lilies from Eton, bound in pale blue silk, and white roses from King's College, bound in purple ribbon. They are left there for 24 hours, and are then taken away and burnt.

At Eton, each Colleger in Hall receives the sum of threepence on 27 February because of two sixteenth-century wills. In 1514, Robert Rede of Burnham left money to provide for mass to be said annually for the repose of his soul, and that of his wife on 27 February ' while the world shall endure '. Each Colleger connected with this annual obit was to receive the sum of twopence. Twenty-one years later, when Provost Roger Lupton died in 1535, his will added a further penny for the Collegers in return for the same service, making threepence in all. This double gift is still annually given.

The Arbor Tree celebration at Aston-on-Clun, in Shropshire, is locally supposed to commemorate an eighteenth-century marriage, though it almost certainly began much farther back in time than that. A large black poplar, known as the Arbor Tree, stands on the crossroads in the centre of the village, and once a year, is decorated with bright flags. Seven or eight long poles are attached to the branches, and from these, the flags are suspended. They are left there all through the year, and are then renewed when 29 May comes round again.

Local tradition says that the custom dates from 1786, when John Marston, the Squire of the village, married Mary Carter on Oak Apple Day. Probably the whole place was decorated for the occasion, and certainly the Tree had its flags. The bride is said to have been so enchanted by the sight of the latter that she gave money to ensure that the custom should be repeated every year for ever. And perhaps she did; but it is perhaps more likely that her gift went, like that of Lady Mowbray at Haxey, to endow and so maintain an already well-established custom rather than to create a new one. This was Oak Apple Day, and nothing is more probable than that the celebration of that anniversary was already usual in Aston long before she came there. It is even possible that the wedding day may have been fixed to co-incide with what had been for a long time a great local occasion of traditional rejoicing.

An odd little ceremony keeps alive the memory of Dr Browne Willis at Fenny Stratford, in Buckinghamshire, on 11 November, which is St Martin's Day. This is the firing of six miniature cannons, known as the Fenny Poppers, which are kept in the church during the year, and are brought outside on 11 November. The Poppers appear to be of some age, but the custom itself is little more than 200 years old, and the same is true of the church itself, which was built only in 1730. It owes its existence to Dr Browne Willis, patron of the living of Bletchley, who, seeing that there was no church at Fenny Stratford, set about collecting the necessary money to build one there, both for the benefit of the local people and to serve as a chapel of ease for Bletchley. He not only gave most generously himself to the funds, but persuaded a good many of the local gentry to contribute by selling space on the church ceiling on which the arms of all those who gave £10, or upwards, would be displayed. These arms are still visible, stretching right across the ceiling.

When the church was completed in 1730, it was dedicated to St Martin, whose feast day was also Dr Willis's birthday. He arranged for the anniversary of the dedication to be marked by a special sermon, and by a village feast in the evening. After his death in 1760, it was decided to add the firing of the little cannon to the day's festivities, because it was he who had presented them to the church. These Fenny Poppers are small, about 7ins high, and weighing about 20lb; they are loaded with gunpowder, and set off from a safe distance by means of a long rod applied to the touch-holes when red hot. On St Martin's Day, they are brought into the churchyard and fired, first at eight o'clock in the morning, then at noon and again at two o'clock, and finally at six in the evening. The Vicar has the privilege of firing the first Popper of the day.

A triangular granite steeple, 50ft tall and visible for miles round, stands on the top of Worvas Hill, near the Cornish St Ives. It is known as Knill's Steeple, or Knill's Mausoleum, and was built in 1782 by John Knill, who was a Collector of Customs in the district. He intended the steeple to serve as his tomb, but this turned out to be impossible, owing to difficulties about consecration, and when he died in London in 1811, he was buried there, in St Andrew's Church in Holborn.

But if he was denied his singular mausoleum, Knill is not likely to be soon forgotten in the place where he had lived and worked for many years. In 1797, he drew up a complicated deed of trust, in which he provided for the perpetual upkeep of his steeple, and also for the quinquennial distribution of a number of gifts and doles for a variety of different people. These charities were to be distributed every five years on St James's Day, 25 July, and included gifts for the best knitter of fishing-nets, the best curer of pilchards for export, money for the best-behaved follower-boys, wedding portions, rewards for those who had successfully brought up a large family without receiving help from the parish – and much else. Ten little girls, the daughters of seamen or tinners, had £5 divided amongst them in return for going up Worvas Hill, dancing before the mausoleum for at least 15 minutes, and then singing the 'Old Hundredth' to the tune used in Knill's time. They, and the fiddler who played for them, were all required to wear white cockades: he was paid £1 for his services.

This distribution came to be known as the Knillian, or the Knillian-games. It was first held in 1801, while John Knill yet lived, and it has gone on ever since. Certain differences in the awards have crept in, as for instance, with the disappearance of the follower-boys owing to the decline of the pilchard fishing, but for the most part, the gifts are practically unchanged. The day itself has become a local festival, to which hundreds of people come to see the children dance, and to see the various awards given. There is a long procession up to the top of the hill in the morning, in which the Mayor and the town officials walk, along with the beneficiaries, and the ten little girls, with their accompanying fiddler. When the dance round the steeple has been performed, and everyone (not only the children) has sung the 'Old Hundredth' and 'Shall Trelawney Die?', the monies are distributed, and the the processions forms up again for the much easier journey down hill. The Knillian next falls due in 1976.

# 11 Doles and Charities

OF DOLES AND KINDLY GIFTS to the needy, some of them very old, there are still a great many yet in force, even today, when so much that was once the responsibility of personal and ecclesiastical charity has been taken over by the State. In the Middle Ages when, in spite of much harshness and cruelty, religion really was the centre of most people's lives, the relief of poverty and distress was considered the first duty of a Christian, and money was generously given, or land bequeathed, for that purpose. In the course of time, many of these medieval gifts were lost or diverted, but some survived and are still given, though often in a slightly modified form.

At Biddenden, in Kent, an ancient dole, known as the Biddenden Dole or the Maids' Charity, is distributed every year at Easter. The date of this charity is very uncertain, and it is now generally agreed that it was probably instituted in the sixteenth century, but long-standing popular belief says it was founded in the twelfth century by twin sisters named Eliza and Mary

Chulkhurst, who left to the parish 20 acres of land, the profits of which were to provide for an annual dole of bread, cheese, and beer for the local poor. This land, still known as the Bread and Cheese Lands, pays now for the distribution of the bread and cheese, but the beer has vanished. It was last heard of in the records of the mid-seventeenth century, but not since. Some years ago, a part of the land was sold to build a housing estate, a change of use which has greatly increased the income of the charity.

Legend says that the two sisters were born in 1100, and that they were joined together from birth by ligaments at the shoulders and the hips. When they reached the age of 34, one died. The friends of the survivor urged her to free herself by having the ligaments cut, but she would not, saying that as they had come together, so they must go together. Six hours later, she too died. This odd story seems at first sight to be supported by the famous Biddenden Cakes, which are distributed at the same times as the Dole. They are really biscuits rather than cakes, very hard and quite uneatable, and each one is marked with the figures of two women who have always been assumed to represent the sisters. They stand very close together, so close that they might easily appear to be joined on one side, and only one arm in each case is visible. Their names appear over their heads and the name of the village beneath their feet. On the

A

apron of one is stamped 34, their supposed age at death, on that

Y

of the other ' in 1100 '. However, Edward Hasted, the historian of Kent, says that the imprint is not by any means as old as it looks, and did not appear on the cakes at all until some 50 years before he wrote his *History and Antiquities of the County of Kent* in 1790. He believes that the figures are not the sisters at all, but two poor widows of a kind most likely to benefit by the Dole. He rejects the story of the joined twins as without any foundation, and says that the givers of the Bread and Cheese Lands were two women named Preston.

The parish records show that this charity has been distributed for at least 300 years, and probably longer. Originally, it was given inside the parish church on Easter Sunday, but after 1682, it was moved to the church porch, and later on to the Old Workhouse. This, now used as two cottages, is still the site of the ceremony, which now takes place on Easter Monday. During the Commonwealth, when the Rector of the parish, George Wilde, was sequestered and his place taken by a Puritan minister named William Horner, the latter laid claim to the Bread and Cheese Lands as part of the glebe lands. This claim was furiously resisted by the churchwardens and the parishioners, and was defeated, twice, for having been defeated in 1646 when the matter was brought before the Kent Commissioners, the obstinate Mr Horner brought it up again in 1656, and lost once more. The Dole was saved, and today genuine claimants still receive gifts of bread and cheese, as of old. The Cakes are given to all present, including the many visitors who come to see the ceremony.

Another medieval charity with an interesting legend is the Tichborne Dole. This consists of flour (formerly loaves of bread) which is annually given on Lady Day (25 March) to the parishioners of Tichborne, Cheriton and Lane End in Hampshire. Tradition has it that this charity was founded by Lady Mabella, the wife of Sir Henry de Tichborne, in the twelfth century. She was a woman renowned for her kindness and generosity all through her life, and was greatly loved by the poor of her own manor. When she was dying, she made a last effort for their welfare by begging her husband to set aside some land from which an annual dole of bread could be provided on Lady Day. His answer was to take a burning brand from the fire and tell her she could have as much land for the purpose of the dole as she could walk round before the flames went out. In her dying state, this practically equalled a refusal, but Lady Mabella was evidently as tough as she was good-hearted. She ordered her maids to carry her outside, and then, since she was unable to walk, she began to crawl as fast as she could over the ground. In this way she covered 23 acres of land, still known as The Crawls, before the flames of the brand failed.

She was taken back to her room, and there, soon afterwards, she died. Before she went, she made her husband promise to fulfil the obligation he had taken on; and she warned him that if he, or any of his descendants, ever stopped the Dole, the family would fall under a curse. Their fortunes would decline and fail, the family name would be changed, and the long-established line would die out. And they would know when all this was about to happen because there would be a generation of seven sons, followed by a generation of seven daughters. After that, the end would come.

For the next six centuries, the dole was faithfully given, but in 1796 Sir Henry Tichborne, then head of the family, stopped it and diverted the revenues of The Crawls to the Church. Sir Henry, in due course, became the father of seven sons; his heir had seven daughters, and if these things were not warnings enough, part of the house fell down. The dole was firmly restored by Sir Henry's third son, Sir Edward Doughty-Tichborne, and has been given without fail ever since. In 1947, it was threatened by the Ministry of Food which, having agreed to supply the bread units still necessary in those days of continued rationing, suddenly refused to do so. When this became known, over 5,000 bread units were voluntarily contributed by members of the public all over the country. In the end, it was not necessary to use them because the Ministry gave way under the pressure of public opinion, and issued the necessary coupons, and those so generously given were gratefully returned to their owners. The Dole now consists of a ton-and-a-half of flour, made from wheat grown on The Crawls, instead of the loaves which were given in earlier times. Before the distribution, there is a short open-air service, conducted by the Chaplain of the household, or sometimes by the Roman Catholic Bishop of Portsmouth, when the flour is blessed, and prayers are offered for the repose of Lady Mabella's soul. The flour is then given out from the steps of the church, one gallon to each man, and half a gallon to each woman and child.

Lady Marvin's charity is still distributed at Ufton Court in Berkshire, on the Friday after the third Sunday in Lent, as it has been since her will of 1583 provided for 169 loaves to be given to the poor of the parish, and nine persons to receive five yards of flannel and 11 yards of calico, or canvas. In the case of the materials, some modernization has been permitted, but otherwise Lady Marvin's gifts continue, and are distributed through a window in the back of the beautiful old house.

Until 1922, a curious charity used to be dispensed in the churchyard of Corfe Mullen, in Dorset, by the stone base of the old cross that was destroyed by Puritan fanatics in 1643. Thomas Phelips, once Lord of the Manor, who died in 1663, left instructions in his will that two pennyworth of bread and two pennyworth of cheese should be given to ten poor persons of the parish on every Sunday of the year. For more than 250 years the food was distributed at the cross, according to Mr Phelips's wish, but since 1922 it has been taken round to the houses of those entitled to receive it. When the income of the charity increased, a third of the money was set aside to pay for a five-year apprenticeship for a boy or a girl; but nowadays, it seems that it is not always easy to find anyone who wants to avail himself (or herself) of this chance.

Many doles are, by the express wish of the donor or for some other reason, given over or by his grave. The Butterworth Charity in London is one of these, though no one now remembers the giver's name, or even the exact situation of his grave. Presumably he lies somewhere in the churchyard of St Bartholomew-the-Great in Smithfield, for it is there that, on Good Friday morning, 21 sixpences are laid upon a flat tombstone, and 21 widows kneel to pick them up, and then step over the stone. Each one afterwards receives half-a-crown (or its modern equivalent) and a hot cross bun. This charity is first mentioned in the churchwardens' accounts for 1686, for which reason it is often assumed that it began then, though there is nothing to show that this is so. All the original documents concerning it have been lost, so that we do not now know the date of the bequest, the name of the donor or where he lies, or even whether he was a man or a woman. The charity is called the Butterworth Charity only because in 1887, when it semed likely to die for lack of funds, it was rescued by Joshua Butterworth, an antiquary of London, who generously gave a sum of money as a perpetual endowment.

On Good Friday, at Ideford, in Devon, the Rector and churchwardens go into the churchyard, and lay out 20 separate shillings on the flat top of Bartholomew Borrington's tomb. They then stand at one end of it, while 20 poor people come, one by one, to the opposite end and pick up their money. This is in accordance with Borrington's will, made in 1585. His wishes have been faithfully fulfilled ever since, except that somehow, in the course of time, the charity has been shifted to Good Friday, instead of being given on Maundy Thursday, as he instructed. Another Elizabethan testator, a London merchant named Peter Symonds, made a will dated 1587, in which he left various Good Friday donations to the poor, together with one item which sheds rather a pleasant light on the man himself, namely a packet of raisins and a new penny for each of the 60 youngest boys at the Bluecoat School (Christ's Hospital). It was his wish that these gifts should be bestowed across his tomb in All Hallows, Lombard Street, and so they were for a long time, but not now; for though most of them (including the raisins and the new penny) are still extant, the tomb itself has disappeared without trace amid the changes of nearly four centuries.

When George Carlow, of Woodbridge in Suffolk, died in 1738, he left directions that loaves of bread to the value of 20s were to be given to the poor from his gravestone on Candlemas Day ' for ever '. This is still regularly done. What is now locally known as Forty Shilling Day is observed at Wootton in Surrey, usually on Candlemas Day also, but sometimes later in the spring, if the wintry weather is very bad. In 1717, William Glanville of Wootton laid it down in his will that, on the anniversary of his death, whenever that might fall, 40s should be given to five poor boys, 16 years old or less, who should go to his tomb on his death date and, laying their hands upon it, recite from memory the Lord's Prayer, the Apostles' Creed, and the Ten Commandments. They were also to read aloud the 15th chapter of the First Epistle of St Paul to the Corinthians, and write out, in a clear hand, two verses of the same chapter. As death finally overtook William Glanville on Candlemas Day, this rather odd ceremony should, and usually does, take place on 2 February. However, the tomb stands outside, in the churchyard, and sometimes it has been necessary to erect a tent over the boys to prevent their being soaked by snow or rain. Also, the recitations and readings take time, and with their hands on the cold stone, the children can become very chilled on a bleak, windy day. Occasionally therefore, during a very cold, wet season, the whole observance has been transferred to a later date, when the weather is likely to be better.

Two interesting charities intended as rewards for good and industrious maidservants exist at Reading and at Guildford. In both, the final decision is curiously arrived at: by the casting of lots at Reading, and by dice-throwing at Guildford. In 1611, John Blagrave of Reading, mathematician and connoisseur of sun-dials, left 20 nobles to be competed for annually by three maidservants, all of whom could prove that they had served faithfully and well in any one Reading household or hostelry for at least five years. They were to go upon Good Friday to the Town Hall, and there cast lots for the money, and so they still do, except that the lot-casting now takes place on the Thursday after Easter and in St Mary's Church House.

In Guildford, John How left £400 in 1674 for the same charitable purpose. The interest on this money was to be given for two years to one of two girls, both good servants in some Guildford house (but not an inn or beerhouse), who cast the highest number when throwing dice. Then, in 1702, John Parsons, another Guildford man, left £600 to benefit some young man just out of his seven-year apprenticeship, who was prepared to go before a magistrate and swear that he was not, at that particular time, worth £20. If it should happen that in a particular year no young man should present himself, then the money should go to some good maidservant who had served satisfactorily for three years together in one house. When, as time went on, the number of apprentice applicants became fewer, and eventually failed alto-gether, the Parsons bequest was absorbed into John How's charity, and the two are now given together every year, in January, at the Guildhall. The girl who throws the highest number receives John How's money, and the Parsons award goes to the second in the contest. As Parsons left more money in the first places, the interest on it is usually higher, so that the loser of the game now stands, rather curiously, to gain more than the winner.

Dice appear also in another bequest, this time for children. Sir Robert Wilde, of St Ives in Huntingdonshire, left £50 in his will drawn up in 1675 to provide for the annual purchase of six Bibles, which were then to be diced for at Whitsuntide by 12 local children. A piece of land was bought, and the rents used to pay for the books; this is still called Bible Orchard, and the St Ives branch of the County Library stands, very appropriately, upon it. Of the 12 children, six are Church of England and six Nonconformist; the testator required that they should all be of 'good repute', and able to read the Bible, and without doubt, they are able, as of old, to fulfil these conditions. The dice-throwing takes place under the direction of the Vicar of the parish. Originally, this contest was held in the church, and the dice were cast upon the altar. About 1880, this practice, came to be considered unsuitable, and instead a table was provided for the purpose by the chancel steps. After 1918, the church school was used for some years, but in 1936, the old custom was restored by the Vicar of the time to the church where it began. Today, the dice are cast, not on the altar, but on the table by the chancel steps which was used before 1918.

A function known as the Peace and Good Neighbourhood Dinner is held in Church Street, Kidderminster, at Midsummer. The roots of this celebration run back a long way , and cannot be very clearly traced to their beginnings. It seems that about 500 years ago an unmarried woman, whose name is not now remembered, left 40s to the inhabitants of Church Street, so that every child born in, or then living in Church Street, might be given a farthing loaf on Midsummer Eve, an anniversary which subsequently came to be locally known as Farthing Loaf Day. She also desired that whoever acted as trustee for this bequest should invite all the men of the street to his house on the same day, so that they might settle any differences that had arisen between them during the past year, and live in peace and amity during the year that followed.

In 1776, a man named John Brecknell, who lived in Church Street himself, added to the original bequest by leaving £150 in his will wherewith to provide an additional gift of a two-penny plum cake for every child or unmarried woman in the street, and also, ale, pipes, and tobacco for the men who attended the Midsummer meeting. In this way, he hoped, as he says in his will, to foster ' the better establishment and continuance of the said Friendly Meeting for Ever '. If any money was left over when everything was paid for, it was to be given to the poor in sums of not more than 5s or less than 2s for each person.

The modern form of all this is the Peace and Good Neighbourhood Dinner, held every year at Midsummer. The chairman opens the proceedings by asking whether any resident of Church Street is at odds with his neighbour, and offering to try to reconcile those concerned, if this should be the case. The main toast of the evening is ' Peace and Good Neighbourhood '; and these words are said when the rest of the united legacies – the loaves, the cakes, and the money for the poor – are distributed to the people of Church Street.

Body-snatchers in the eighteenth and early nineteenth centuries were responsible for several rather strange bequests. The dread that the grave of some dear relative might be broken into and the body stolen, or the fear of the same thing happening in the future to oneself, was very prevalent, and some testators tried to prevent it, as far as they could, by particular clauses in their wills. When Mary Gibson died in 1773, she left money to the Bluecoat School on condition that the Governors went every year to Sutton in Surrey, there to inspect her tomb and satisfy themselves that it had not been disturbed. Similarly, in 1795, when Richard Johnson provided for a sermon to be preached in Hendon Church on the depressing text, ' Human Life is but a bubble ', he arranged for members of the Stationers' Company to attend and hear it, and afterwards to go out and inspect his grave. In Oxford, in 1714, Ann Kendall, one of three sisters living there, left £920 in trust to provide £4 annually for six poor widows or single women of St Thomas's Parish, and a further £4 to pay for a Christmas sermon, on condition that her grave, and that of her parents, should be kept safe from body-snatchers, and never moved from St Thomas's churchyard. The benefactions were to be paid quarterly, and there is a curious legend that the three sisters returned every Quarter Day, presumably to see that their wishes were fulfilled. They were seen walking along the streets all round their old house, sometimes singly and sometimes together. It is said that their appearances were so regular that the people of the district came to expect them as a matter of course. This haunting went on until, in the 1870s, their house on Gloucester Green, which had long been empty, was pulled down. This seemed to sever their last tie to this earth, for they have not been seen since. The legacies endure, however, and are now mainly devoted to educational benefits.

A charity which began as bread and ended up as coal was that locally known as Taynton Cobbs. In 1783, Lady Talbot of Barrington directed in her will that barley from her estates was to be made up into a number of small loaves, called cobbs, and distributed to ' such of the poor children of Burford as attended ' Taynton Church on St Thomas's Day. On that day, formerly, a number of people used to congregate in Burford High Street very early in the morning, before it was light, and march off in procession to Taynton. They carried horns and trumpets and tin trays, and anything else that would make a cheerful, if not a musical, noise as they went, very much in the manner of Teddy Rowe's Band at Sherborne. A sermon used to be preached in the church, and afterwards the cobbs were thrown from the top of the tower to be scrambled for by the children, but this had to be given up because of the noise and disturbance that they made.

Instead, those entitled to receive the cobbs were required to walk through a narrow gateway and be given the loaves there. Now, however, the charity has been changed to an annual allowance of coal, and there is no more ceremony and no more excitement.

Herrings are still distributed at Clavering in Essex in accordance with the will of John Thakes, who in 1537 directed that a barrel of white herrings and a cade of red herrings were to be given to the poor of the parish during Lent. At Sherfield-on-Loddon in Hampshire a rather more than usually imaginative bequest known as Mr Piggot Conant's Charity provides a Christmas dinner of beef and pudding for anyone in the parish who is too poor to buy it himself, and applies for it as ' an indigent person '. In the same county, at Ellingham, eight poor people receive the rents and profits of some land called the Poor's Allotment, bestowed upon them by the will of Dame Elizabeth Tipping in 1687, on St Thomas's Day. This is an anniversary which has always had a great significance for the charitable, for it was then, until well towards the end of the nineteenth century, that poor women in the country ' went a-Thomassing ', (or a-gooding, or mumping, or curning). They went from house to house asking for alms, and expected to receive from each person a pint or a quart of wheat, with which to make loaves or cakes or puddings for their family's Christmas feasting. Sometimes money was given instead, though not very often, and some farmers occasionally gave a piece of meat, but corn was by far the most usual. No one ever refused to give at all, and the more kindly householders often refreshed the Thomassers with hot spiced ale, to keep out the cold. The miller's contribution was to grind the wheat received into flour without charge. On their side, the women usually returned very real good wishes, and a sprig of luck-bringing holly or mistletoe. In the days when wages were very low, Thomassing was a real help to families living on small incomes, and no one then felt that it was begging. With the coming of better times, the custom declined, and is now unknown, but a number of fixed charities are, like that of Dame Elizabeth Tipping, still distributed on St Thomas's Day.

A very charming custom which does not spring from a bequest, and is not at all old – though it has roots running back into the Middle Ages – is the Oranges and Lemons ceremony held on, or about, 31 March, at St Clement Danes Church in London. This began in 1920, after the famous bells had been restored and

L

rededicated the previous year. They had been silent since 1913 because their oak frame was unsafe, and the children's ceremony was instituted by the Rev. William Pennington-Bickford, then Rector of the parish, as a thanksgiving for their return. The church was ornamented with oranges and lemons given by the Danish colony in London, whose church this was originally, and every child who attended the service received one of both these fruits. The bells and the church were alike seriously damaged in 1941 during World War II, but afterwards the building was restored and became the Royal Air Force church, and the bells were rehung in 1957.

Now, on 31 March, the anniversary of the first ceremony in 1920, or as near to it as may be convenient, the children of the nearby school all go to a short service in the church, and one of them reads the lesson. The sermon and the blessing are given by the Royal Air Force Chaplain. ' Oranges and Lemons say the bells of St Clements' is played at the end of the service on handbells, as four times a day it is now rung on the famous bells above; and as the children flock out of the building, each one is given an orange and a lemon by the Chaplain and his helpers.

Apart from the nursery rhyme, the parish of St Clement Danes has a very long association with oranges and lemons. When this fruit was first imported into England in the Middle Ages, it was brought up the river in barges from the Pool of London, and landed – or so tradition says – near the churchyard, which then ran down to the Thames. Porters carried them through Clement's Inn on the way to Clare Market, and had to pay toll for the right to pass. A custom which used to obtain in Clement's Inn itself until almost within living memory may perhaps commemorate this medieval trade. On New Year's Day, all the tenants of the inn were visited by the attendants and presented with an orange and a lemon, in return for which they were given half-a-crown.

An ancient charity, which in one form or another has been in existence for more than 800 years, is the Wayfarers' Dole that is still given daily at St Cross Hospital near Winchester. This house was founded in 1136 by Henry de Blois as a home and refuge for 13 poor men, where they could be provided ' with garments and beds suitable for their infirmities, good wheaten bread daily of the weight of 5 marks, and three dishes at dinner, and one at supper suitable to the day, and drink of good stuff '.

Then, in 1446, Cardinal Beaufort added another almshouse, that of Noble Poverty, for men of higher rank who had fallen on evil times through no fault of their own. Both these foundations exist today, running side by side, separate, but under one head. The original poor men, the Blois Brethren, wear black gowns with the silver cross of the Knights Hospitallers of St John upon them, and the Beaufort Brethren wear dark-red gowns and the Cardinal's hat badge. All alike receive free housing, food allowance, and pocket money.

From its beginnings, the hospital has been a centre of widespread charity. In Henry de Blois's day, a hundred poor persons were fed there every day, and some 50 years later, this number was raised to 200. Today, the Wayfarers' Dole is given without question to the first 32 persons who ask for it at the porter's lodge on any one day. It consists of a piece of white bread, served on an old carved wooden platter and a draught of ale in a horn bearing the arms of the Order. No conditions are laid down, and no reasons for needing the Dole have to be given. Whoever asks may receive. The only difference made between one person and another is that those who are really in want are given a larger portion.

# 12 Wakes and Fairs

IN MANY PARISHES STILL, the Patronal Festival of the church is celebrated by a local holiday known as the Wake (or Wakes), the Feast, or the Revel. The name varies with the district in which the holiday is held, Wakes being mainly found in the northern and midland counties, Revels in the Westcountry, and Feasts elsewhere. The Patronal Festival is, of course, primarily a religious anniversary, held on the feast day of the saint in whose name the church is dedicated, or on the anniversary of the dedication ceremony. In earlier times, it was customary for the people to watch and pray during the night, or part of it, and it is from this practice, now long since vanished, that the name 'Wake' derives.

Because Wakes and Feasts are dependent upon the varying dates of church dedications, they may be found at different times in different places. In 1536, an Act of Convocation required every parish to keep its Wakes on the same day, the first Sunday in October, regardless of the local saint's feast day, or the dedication anniversary; but this mandate was a failure from the beginning. In all but a few villages, the old ways quietly continued, and the Wakes were celebrated as before, on the Patronal Festival, or in some places, on a customary day at the end of hay or corn harvest.

Before the Reformation, when the people had watched, or 'waked', in the church by night and heard Mass in the morning, they spent the rest of the day in sports and games and jollifications of all sorts. When the watching and attendance at Mass were given up, they still kept up their happy celebrations, going to church first in the morning, and then turning whole-heartedly to feasting, dancing, racing, and every kind of merrymaking. This was the day (or days, for the Wakes sometimes went on for several, occasionally for as much as a week), of all the year, when country people entertained their town friends and relations. The annual rush bearing usually took place during the Wakes, and so did bull- and bear-baiting until both were made illegal in 1835. Even after that date, they continued for some years, if not openly, then in some hidden place, where the people could watch the sport they loved without being observed by outsiders, and the parish constable pretended not to notice this breaking of the law. At Bunbury in Cheshire, for instance, baiting went on without any attempt at concealment until 1848, and thereafter continued secretly for a time in a safe corner of the nearby Delamere Forest.

Entertainers of various kinds, including musicians, came to provide amusement for the parishioners and their guests, and the people who came in from outside to see the fun. Among the musicians in later times, and until the outbreak of the World War I, were the German bands who used to come to England at the beginning of the summer, and travel about from village to village, playing at Wakes and similar festivities, until the time came for them to return to Germany in the autumn. Bear-baiting slowly died out as the laws against it began to bite more fiercely, but the dancing bears still came round, with their bearwards, until well towards the end of Edward VII's reign. There were also pedlars, and travelling salesmen, who set up stalls and booths in the village street, and for the time being turned it into the semblance of a little fair. Most of this has gone now, but Wakes and Feasts are still gaily celebrated in many parishes, though they are no longer as lively as they once were. In the industrial towns of Lancashire and Yorkshire, the name 'Wakes' now denotes a week's or a fortnight's holiday, when the mills and factories are closed for cleaning, and the furnaces are drawn. Nearly all the workers go away for the holiday – to Blackpool once, but now, more probably to Spain – but there are local gaieties also for those who prefer to stay at home.

Sometimes the local Wakes or Feast grew in the course of time into a Fair, and sometimes it assumed the name of Fair without any real right except that of custom. One of these is St Giles's Fair in Oxford, which began as Walton Wakes, and is now one of the best-known pleasure fairs in the southern Midlands. The Manor of Walton originally lay outside the city walls, and belonged in the Middle Ages to the Abbey of Godstow, passing after the dissolution of the monasteries to St John's College, Oxford. It held its Wake on the Monday and Tuesday after the first Sunday after 1 September, the feast day of St Giles who is the patron saint of the parish. 'At present we have no Fair ', wrote Sir John Peshall in his *Antient and Present State of Oxford*, in 1773, 'a Wake is at S. Giles, called S. Giles's Wake, yearly, the Monday after S. Giles's day.' He was not quite correct about the date of the Wake, but he was right about Oxford having no fair. In the strict sense, it has not got one now, for what we now call St Giles's Fair never acquired a charter, and the other five fairs of the city, all of them chartered, have one by one disappeared.

At one period in its history, St Giles's Fair did an enormous trade in cloth, crockery, ironware, gloves, cheese, and agricultural produce, and traders came to it from all over the country. Some of these things are sold there today, though only in small quantities. It has, however, now become mainly a pleasure fair. It is still held on its old ground, on what used to be St Giles's Field, and is now one of the main streets leading northwards out of the city, and also Magdalen Street. No so long ago, it was the custom for Oxford people to go on Fair Monday to ' See the Fair in ' at five o'clock in the morning. Great crowds would assemble to see the machines racing on to their allotted places, and going into action as quickly as possible. By half-past six, normally, some of the coconut shies and swinging boats were well away, and by eleven o'clock, most of the bigger shows were already in full swing and doing a roaring trade.

Of the true fairs, established by royal charter, the majority run back to the time of the Normans, who created many new fairs, and also legalized, by the bestowal of charters, fairs which had existed before the Conquest. Some of our most ancient surviving fairs may well be much older than their charters. Alfred the Great founded several of these, and there are others which began long before his day. Cornelius Walford, in *Fairs, Past and Present* (1883), traces Helston Fair back to Roman times, as well as some that still exist, or did until recently, along the line of the Roman Wall in Northumberland. Weyhill Fair in Hampshire, which unhappily faded away during the last few years, received its charter in the eleventh century, but was traditionally said to have been in existence long before that. It was a great sheep fair in its heyday, and also sold horses, hops and cheeses; merchants flocked to the site on 10 October from far and near. From first (whenever that may have been) to last – which was only recently – it is claimed that it has always been held on the same ground, on a site at the boundary of three parishes where two very ancient roadways crossed. These were the Tin Road from Cornwall, and the Gold Road from North Wales, along which Irish gold was brought to the south coast, for further transport to the Continent. One part of the ground was always known as Gold Street. It is possible – and indeed probable – that some sort of unofficial fair or market was held there from early times at this important meeting-place, and the charter granted in the eleventh century merely gave it legal status. It was at Weyhill Fair that the well-known wife-selling incident in Hardy's *The Mayor of Casterbridge* is supposed to have taken place.

A curious custom used to be kept up on the night before the Fair until about 1890. At the Star Inn, a pair of ram's horns with a metal cup fixed between them were once kept, and possibly still are. On the eve of the Fair, a Horn Supper was held, and newcomers were initiated in a ceremony known as Horning the Colt. The novice was seated in a chair, and the horns were placed on his head, the cup between them being filled with ale. The company then sang:

> So swift runs the fox, so cunning runs the fox,
> Why shouldn't this heifer grow up to be an ox?
> And get his living among the briars and thorns,
> And drink like his daddy with a large pair of horns,
>     Horns, boys, horns, boys, horns,
> And drink like his daddy with a large pair of horns.

The newcomer then drank the ale in the cup, and paid his footing by treating the company to half a gallon of ale.

In the Middle Ages, fairs were the great trading events of the year. Some of the more important attracted merchants not only from every part of England, but also from France, Germany, Flanders, and elsewhere in Europe. They brought enormous revenues to their owners, and golden opportunities of profit and pleasure to those who came to them. While they lasted, the normal Guild regulations forbidding outsiders to trade within a city or borough were suspended, and strangers were free to enter and sell their goods until the fair ended. An Act of 1331 ordered that ' every Lord at the beginning of his Fair shall proclaim how long the fair shall endure ', and fixed stern penalties for anyone who continued to buy and sell after it was over. In medieval Chester, during the great Midsummer Fair which began on 24 June and ran for three days, all trade of any kind, other than that which took place on the fairground outside the Abbey gates was strictly forbidden, and even the ships on the river were obliged to remain unloaded for as long as the fair lasted. As Chester was a considerable trading-port until the silting-up of the river Dee made it impossible for sea-going vessels to reach it, this must have been exceedingly exasperating for all those concerned, but there was no help for it.

While a fair was running, the regular courts of the borough concerned were superseded by the Court of Pie Powder, the ' court of dusty feet ', which had jurisdiction over all matters connected with the fair and those who came to it. These courts had the great advantage that disputes and actions for debts, trespass, assault, and the like could be settled on the spot by merchants better able than any outsider to judge and understand the people with whom they had to deal. A statute of 1478 speaks of such courts as pertaining of right to a fair, and goes on to say :

> In which courts it hath been all times accustomed that every person coming to the same fairs, should have lawful remedy of all manner of contracts, trespasses, convenants, debts, and other deeds made or done within any of the same fairs and within the jurisdiction of the same, and to be tried by merchants being of the same fair.

The benefit to itinerant traders and others of being able to have their cases settled immediately, without having to wait for the Assizes, and perhaps having to travel a long way back to them from whatever place they might have moved to by then, was obviously very great. Such courts continued for a long time, though they died out gradually as the fairs themselves declined in importance, and many lapsed after the passing of the County Courts Act in 1888. A few still remain, as for instance, at the ' Dirty ', or October, Fair at Market Drayton, or at St Bartholomew's Fair at Newbury.

The old signal that the Guild Laws were temporarily suspended and that, therefore, strangers might safely enter and trade, was a wooden Hand or Glove, displayed in some prominent place. So long as the Hand or Glove remained visible, so long was the fair deemed to be running, and outsiders might play their part in it without fear of arrest or punishment. At Honiton Fair, which has existed at least since 1221, and received a charter in 1257, the Town Crier walks up the main street to the Old Market House, carrying a tall pole garlanded with flowers, at the top of which is a large gilt glove, made of leather and stuffed with straw. At noon, he rings his bell, and then cries out loudly, and repeats each part of the proclamation three times:

> Oyez! Oyez! Oyez!
> The Glove is up and the Fair is begun!
> No man shall be arrested
> Until the Glove is taken down!
>
> God Save The Queen!

A gathering of children shouts out the words after him, and then they all scramble for a shower of hot pennies, which are thrown to them from the upper windows of the Angel and the King's Arms hotels. This fair, after several changes of date during the course of its long life, is now held on the Tuesday and Wednesday after 19 July. During these two days, the Glove is prominently displayed, as is another, also stuffed and garlanded with flowers, at Barnstaple September Fair.

In Chester, it was not a Glove but a wooden Hand which was displayed to mark the duration of the summer and autumn fairs. It used to be hung from the roof of St Peter's Church, near Chester Cross, and was last hung there about the middle of last century. A collector who apparently acquired it about that time subsequently left it to the Corporation of Liverpool.

An old chartered fair at St Ives in Huntingdonshire has the odd distinction of being older than the name of the town to which it belongs. It was granted by Henry I in 1110 to the Abbey of Ramsey which at that time owned the little township of Slepe. Here was buried St Ive, or Ivo, a saint who must not be confused with the patron of the other St Ives in Cornwall, whose real name was Ia, and who is traditionally said to have floated across from Ireland to Cornwall on a cabbage leaf. The Huntingdonshire man was a Persian bishop who is alleged to have become a hermit in that country. When his bones were moved to Slepe, a healing spring arose near his grave, and later when, largely through the effects of the fair, Slepe grew very considerably in size, it took the name of St Ives. In the thirteenth century, this was one of England's greatest fairs, trading chiefly in cloth, wool, and hides, but like the even greater, and slightly older fair at Winchester, it declined during the Hundred Years' War, and the years that followed. Originally it was held at Easter and lasted for eight days, but by Edward II's reign, it had been extended to over 40 days, and ended on Whitsun Eve. All that is now left of St Ives's great fair tradition is a market on Whit Monday, and a single-day pleasure fair on the Tuesday nearest 11 October.

A medieval fair of equal, or even greater commercial importance was that held in Sturbridge, a field just outside Cambridge. King John gave it a charter in 1211, but tradition says that it began long before then in the time of the Roman emperor, Carausius. Daniel Defoe, writing in the early eighteenth century, speaks of a turnover of as much as £100,000 there in the course of a single week, and describes how, while it lasted, the field became like a busy town, where almost anything that anyone could possibly desire could be easily obtained. It ran from Bartholomew-tide until noon on Michaelmas Day. On 24 August (the Feast of St Bartholomew), a very splendid procession set out from Cambridge, with music and trumpeters, drums and banners, to proclaim the opening of the fair. After the ceremony, there was a grand banquet, at which fresh herring was the traditional main dish.

Defoe tells us that 'the fair is like a well fortify'd city, and there was a grand banquet, at which fresh herring was the seen anywhere, with so great a concourse of people '. But the ' fortifications ' and the good management could not keep this very old fair going for long after the end of the eighteenth century. Nevertheless, it was proclaimed every year by the Mayor of Cambridge, to steadily diminishing audiences, until 1933. In her *Byways of Cambridge History*, Mrs Keynes relates how, on that last occasion, she, being Mayor at the time, went with the Clerk of the Peace and the Sergeant-at-arms and proclaimed the old fair once more, to an audience of two women, two babies, and an ice-cream barrow. Sturbridge Fair was ended at last.

At Sherborne in Dorset the fair held on the Monday after 10 October, Old Michaelmas Day, is really St Michael's Fair, but it is far better known by its secondary name of Pack Monday Fair. Until very recently, it was always ushered in by an unusual and noisy custom known as Teddy Rowe's Band. Very early in the morning of Fair Day, as soon as possible after midnight, a crowd of young people of both sexes marched through the streets beating tin trays, frying-pans, and dustbin-lids, blowing horns and whistles, and generally making as much strident and discordant noise as possible. They paraded thus through the sleeping town, calling themselves Teddy Rowe's Band, and claimed to have done the same on Fair Day morning for the last 500 years without a break.

Legend says that the original Teddy Rowe or Roe was the foreman employed by Abbot Peter Ramsam in the late fifteenth century in the construction of the great fan vault in the nave of the abbey church. In 1490, the work was finished, and the workmen were given a holiday and told to go out and enjoy themselves. Out they went, therefore, and, led by Teddy Rowe, marched in triumph through the town, shouting, blowing horns, and making every kind of loud and cheerful noise. This, apparently, was the origin of the early morning parade on the morning of Pack Monday Fair. Local tradition also has it that the fair's name sprang from the masons' packing their goods and subsequently departing from the town.

Whatever the truth of the explanation may be, there is no doubt that the custom persisted for several centuries, and no one seems to have objected to it very seriously, in spite of being awakened by hideous noises in the darkness of early morning. Attempts have been made to suppress it from time to time, but without success. Now, however, it seems to have fallen a victim to that curse of our age, hooliganism. In 1964, it was banned by the police because of damage to property and general hooliganism, and this ban has been renewed yearly ever since.

Mitcham Fair lacks a charter that can be traced, though there is a strong local belief that Elizabeth I did, in fact, grant a fair to the town in 1598. But the charter concerning this cannot be found, although a great search was made for it in 1923, at the time of the passing of the Mitcham Urban District Council Act. Neither the Record Office nor the British Museum knew of it, nor could the Showmen's Guild produce it. Nevertheless, the 'Golden Key', 4½ft long, huge and gilded, which the Mayor holds up for the people to see at the opening ceremony, is firmly referred to in the official guide as 'The Chartered Key of Mitcham'. The fair is now held on 12 August and the two following days on Three Kings Green, and is said to be one of the most flourishing in the London area.

Another fair to which Queen Elizabeth is sometimes said to have granted a charter, though she did not, is the celebrated Pole Fair at Corby in Northamptonshire. This takes place every 20 years, traditionally on Whit Monday, and is next due in 1982. It is sometimes called the Charter Fair, not because it possesses such a thing in its own right, but because, on that occasion a charter is commemorated which Queen Elizabeth bestowed upon Corby in 1585, and Charles II confirmed in 1682. Legend has it that when she was staying nearby in Sir Christopher Hatton's house, Kirby Hall, her horse bolted with her one day and threw her into a bog. Some workmen rushed to her rescue, and in gratitude for their promptness and courage, she bestowed the charter on the town. This relieved the inhabitants from certain toll payments and from some jury and militia services, but it did not give them a fair. There does not appear to be any particular evidence for this romantic story, which bears a strong resemblance to the legend told of Lady Mowbray in relation to the Haxey Hood Game, but the charter remains, and is regularly read out at the opening ceremony, in the presence of the rector and the town officers.

The name 'Pole Fair' arises from an odd custom for which no explanation is readily forthcoming, but which still flourishes, as it seems to have done for an uncertain but probably lengthy period. Before the festivities of the day begin, all the roads leading into the town are barred with wooden gates, and anyone wishing to enter is required to pay a toll. If he refuses, he is mounted on a pole and carried off to one of the three sets of stocks still standing in the town. There he is given another chance, but if he still declines to pay up, he is put in the stocks and left there until he relents. The same treatment is meted out to women, except that they are carried in a chair, and not astride a pole. Appeals to the police are quite useless, for this is Corby's great day, and to act thus once in 20 years is their immemorial privilege. Moreover, it is not only strangers who are so treated, for anyone in the streets, old or young, man or woman, is liable to be seized and imprisoned, and made to pay ransom like any incomer. There is no doubt that the whole thing is regarded as an enormous frolic by the townsmen, and that many people deliberately put themselves in the way of capture for the fun of sitting in the stocks, like an old-time malefactor, and perhaps having their photographs taken therein. For anyone who strongly objects to these lively practices – and admittedly, it is a little startling for an unwarned traveller to find himself thus suddenly involved in a medieval antic – there does not appear to be any real remedy except resignation and a pocketful of small change, or else keep away from the place altogether on this historic day.

Widecombe Fair is known all over the English-speaking world because of the famous song which is named after it. This song is now firmly fixed in almost everybody's mind as belonging to Widecombe-in-the-Moor in Devon, but in fact other versions of it were known well before the Rev. Sabine Baring-Gould published this one in 1890, in his *Songs of the West*. In some of these, other fairs are mentioned, such as Tavistock, or Helston, or, in a Somerset song collected by Cecil Sharp, a ' Midsummer Fair ' which has no place-name attached to it. As far as Widecombe Fair itself is concerned, little is known of its history, and its age is uncertain, though it is not usually thought to be very old – as fairs reckon age. It takes place in September, and has a small but vigorous trade in Dartmoor ponies and sheep, and a large annual influx of holidaymakers and tourists. One character mentioned in the song – Uncle Tom Cobley – does seem to have existed, and to have had some connection with the Widecombe district. This was Thomas Cobley, a wealthy local farmer, who died in 1794 at the ripe old age of 96 and is buried in Spreyton churchyard.

At Ebernoe, in Sussex, a Horn Fair is held every year on
25 July, and has been, according to local tradition, for a number
of centuries. It is noted for two things – a roasted sheep and a
cricket match – the horns and mask of the former serving as a
trophy to be won by the victors in the latter. A horned sheep is
roasted whole in a pit in the ground just outside the boundary
of the cricket field. Its head and horns project over the edge
so as to preserve them from the effects of heat, and while it is
slowly cooking on the morning of Fair Day, visitors baste the
meat, for good luck. When the sheep is thoroughly roasted, the
head is cut off. During the afternoon, there is a cricket match
between Ebernoe and a team from some parish in the neighbourhood, at the end of which the horns and mask of the sheep are
presented to that member of the winning team who has scored
the most runs. Nobody knows the origin of this singular custom,
nor how old it is, but of its present popularity and probable
continuance for a long time to come, there can be little doubt.

Once, there was another Horn Fair of a decidedly more
boisterous character, which was held at Charlton in Kent on St
Luke's Day, 18 October. At this fair, horns were to be seen everywhere. Men wore them on their heads, the gingerbread fairings
were stamped with them, and every stall was surmounted by a
gilded pair. There was a local saying that ' All's Fair at Horn
Fair ' which was held to account for and condoned every sort of
horse-play and rowdiness. Men often wore women's clothes, and
amused themselves by running about the fairground and striking
every female they met with sprigs of furze. Until about 1770,
a noisy procession used to set out from an inn in Bishopgate,
consisting of a king and a queen, a miller and his wife, and a
large number of men and women all wearing horns, who marched
cheerfully off to Charlton, eight miles away, and there paraded
three times round the church.

The legend locally told to account for these odd customs, and
for the fair itself, is scandalous and quite without foundation.
It is said that when King John was staying in his palace at
Eltham, he went hunting over Shooter's Hill on St Luke's
Day and, needing refreshment, stopped at the house of a miller
in search of hospitality. The miller was absent, and the King
amused himself by making love to his wife. The miller, returning
suddenly, threatened to kill both him and his own wife, but was
eventually pacified by a royal gift, not only of an estate nearby,

but also of a fair, to be held every year on St Luke's Day. For this slanderous story, there is no evidence whatever; in fact, King John never granted a fair to Charlton, and though his son, Henry III, did so in 1268, this was at Trinity-tide, and not in October, and had in any case ceased to exist before the middle of the seventeenth century. There is, of course, a far simpler explanation for this charterless fair and its horns, for 18 October is St Luke's Day, and St Luke was the patron saint of Charlton parish. It is probable that the Horn Fair held on that day was really the Wakes holiday, grown and extended. Moreover, the saint's emblem is a horned ox, so that it would be quite natural that, as the fair grew in popularity, that horns should become more prominent as its chief symbol. It is perhaps also natural that, in the course of time, a lively and ribald story should spring up amongst the people, and be freely adopted in place of the sober and half-forgotten facts.

The so-called Fairlop Fair in Hainault Forest began in the early eighteenth century when Daniel Day, a blockmaker of Wapping who owned property in the forest region, came to collect his rents on the first Friday in July. As a way of enlivening the occasion, it was his pleasant custom to give a dinner of beans and bacon to his friends and tenants under the spreading branches of a giant oak tree known as the Fairlop Oak. This purely private jollification became extremely popular, and slowly grew, first into a distribution of bacon and beans to all and sundry from beneath the oak, and then into a sort of unofficial fair. Pedlars, entertainers, and the owners of shows were attracted to it, stalls of various kinds sprang up round the tree, and by 1725, all the fun and business of a real fair were to be found there.

Day lived to be 84 years old and died, highly respected by all who knew him, in 1767. For several years before his death, the blockmakers of Wapping honoured him by sending 30 or 40 of their number to Fairlop Fair every year. They travelled in a long boat made from a single block of firwood, which was mounted upon a cart, or lorry, and drawn by six strong horses. It was decorated with flags and coloured streamers, and was preceded by a band of musicians. When a branch of the oak was blown off in a gale, Day had his coffin made from it, and carefully lay down in it when it was finished, to be sure that it was not too short. The fair continued after his death, and also survived the fall of the famous tree, blown down during a violent storm in 1820. Finally, after almost 150 years of cheerful life, Fairlop Fair was abolished in 1835 by order of the Commissioners of Woods and Forests.

Some Fairs are named after their principal merchandise, past or present. There is a great Sheep Fair at Corby (in Lincoln-shire), and a Cheese Fair at Frome, where the cheeses are often dipped in a stream at the start, for luck. The secondary name of Cambridge Midsummer Fair is Pot Fair, since pottery and horses were for a long time its main trading commodities. Nottingham Goose Fair, now mainly a pleasure-fair, really was a Goose Fair once, when many thousands of geese were driven in from the surrounding countryside and sold on its wide fair-ground. This fair was a fine sight when it was held in the splendid market place of the city, but since 1928, it has been moved to an open space called the Forest, about a mile from the town centre. In its medieval heyday, it ran for 21 days, but now it is a three-day event, beginning on the first Thursday in October.

There are still numerous horse fairs, particularly in the northern counties. At Appleby, in June, there is a famous Gypsy Horse Fair. Gypsies come pouring into the town from an immensely wide area, with their painted caravans and their beautiful horses. About a thousand caravans gather round Fair Hill, and along the roads leading to it for about two miles. Brough Hill Fair in Yorkshire was, and still is, another meeting-place for gypsies, and it was here that the Durham mine-owners came to buy their pit ponies. The best-known horse fair in the south is that which takes place in September at Barnet. At one time immense numbers of cattle were sold there also but, when the introduction of root foods and the invention of refrigerators made it unnecessary for thousands of cattle to be slaughtered every autumn, that part of the trade disappeared. The horses remained, and though their numbers have by now sunk from thousands to hundreds, the Horse Fair, as such, is still a very lively and popular event.

The statute (or mop, or hiring) fairs, which still exist in a number of places, chiefly in the Midlands, are now usually pleasure fairs, but until the beginning of this century, they still served a very useful purpose. It was long customary for farm servants, indoor or outdoor, to be engaged by the year, and then, if they wanted to change or their master did not re-engage them, to seek new places at the local hiring fair. They stood in an allotted part of the fairground, bearing some recognizable token of their calling, such as a tuft of wool, or a crook for a shepherd, a piece of horsehair or a whip for a carter, a pail or some cowhair for a milkmaid, and so on. When they had been engaged, they received a ' fastenpenny ' – a small coin to seal the bargain – and then they went off to enjoy themselves at the fair for the rest of the day.

The hiring, or ' stattit ' fair grew up gradually from the statute sessions, which in their turn, owed their being to the various Statutes of Labourers enacted between the reign of Edward III and that of Elizabeth I. By these Acts, the justices of the peace were empowered to fix the rate of wages, and required to proclaim these rates at the sessions held in market towns, usually at Michaelmas or Martinmas, but sometimes at Whitsuntide, or on Old May Day. When Elizabeth I repealed the Statutes of Labourers, she retained the sessions because they had proved to be so useful. Workers and employers of the neighbourhood came to these gatherings to hear what they would receive, or what they would have to pay, and naturally entered into hiring agreements with each other on the spot. And since there was here a considerable gathering of people, there came, equally naturally, sellers of food and drink, gingerbread and fairings, and eventually the providers of amusement; and so grew up the fair.

Sometimes when the newly engaged servant got to his new place, he did not like it, or his master did not like him. In many places, there was a second hiring day about a week or a fortnight later, to which either or both could go and try again. This second fair was called the Runaway Mop, a name which still survives in some districts, attached to fairs now mainly concerned with pleasure. In Bicester, formerly, matters were even easier, for there were three opportunities available – first the Hiring Fair itself on the Friday following Old Michaelmas Day : then the Runaway Fair, a week later, and finally, the Confirmation Fair, a further week later, by which time even the most exacting would have been suited.

M

# Select Bibliography

ADDISON, W., English Fairs and Markets, 1953.
ADDY, S. O., Household Tales, with Other Traditional Remains collected in the Counties of York, Lincoln, Derby, and Nottingham, 1895.
ALFORD, V., 'The Abbots Bromley Horn Dance', *Antiquity*, June, 1933.
———, Introduction to English Folklore, 1952.
ANDREWS, W., Curious Church Customs, 1895.
ATKINSON, J. C., Forty Years in a Moorland Parish, 1891.
AUBREY, J. Remaines of Gentilisme and Judaisme, ed, J. Britten, 1881.

BALFOUR, M. C., & THOMAS, N. W., Northumberland. *County-Folk-Lore*. Vol. IV, 1904.
BARING-GOULD, SABINE, Old Country Life, 1890.
BEDDINGTON, W., and CHRISTY, E., It Happened in Hampshire, n.d.
BIDDENDEN LOCAL HISTORY SOCIETY, The Story of Biddenden, 1953.
BILLSON, C. J., Leicestershire & Rutland. *County Folk-Lore*, Vol. 1, 1895.
BLOOM, J. HARVEY, Folk Lore, Old Customs and Superstitions in Shakespeareland, 1929.
BRAND, J., Observations on the Popular Antiquities of Great Britain, ed. Sir Henry Ellis, 1849.
BRAY, MRS. A. E., The Borders of the Tamar and the Tavy, 2nd, ed. 1879.
BURNE, C. S., Shropshire Folk-Lore, 1883.

CARKEET-JAMES, COL E. H., His Majesty's Tower of London, 1950.
CAUDWELL, I., Ceremonies of Holy Church, 1948.
CHAMBERS, R., The Book of Days, 1864.
CHESHIRE SHEAF, THE., Reprinted from the Chester Courant.

COURTNEY, M. A., Cornish Feasts and Folk-Lore, 1890.

DACOMBE, M. R., Dorset Up Along and Down Along, n.d.
DENHAM, M. A., The Denham Tracts, ed. J. Hardy, 1892, 1895, 2 vols.
DERBYSHIRE NOTES & QUERIES.
DEVON AND CORNWALL NOTES & QUERIES.
DEVONSHIRE ASSOCIATION, Transactions of the.
DITCHFIELD, P. H., Old English Customs, 1896.
DYER, T. THISTLETON, British Popular Customs, 1876.

EDWARDS, T. J., Military Customs, 1961.

FOLKLORE, Journal of the Folklore Society.
FRAZER, SIR J. G., The Golden Bough, 1913-15.

GLOUCESTERSHIRE NOTES AND QUERIES.
GURDEN, LADY CAMILLA, Suffolk, *County Folk-Lore*, Vol. 1, 1893.
GUTCH, M., The North Riding of Yorkshire, York, and the Ainsty. *County Folk-Lore*, Vol. II, 1899.
——,The East Riding of Yorkshire. *County Folk-Lore*, Vol. VI, 1912.
GUTCH, M., and PEACOCK, M., Folklore concerning Lincolnshire, *County Folk-Lore*, Vol. V, 1908.

HARDWICK, C., History of the Borough of Preston, 1857.
——, Traditions, Superstitions, and Folklore, 1872.
HARLAND, J., and WILKINSON, T. T., Lancashire Folk-Lore, 1867.
HARTLAND, E. S., Gloucestershire. *County Folk-Lore*, Vol. 1, 1895.
HENDERSON, W., Notes on the Folk-Lore of the Northern Counties of England and the Borders, 2nd ed., 1879.
HOLE, C., Traditions and Customs of Cheshire, 1937.
——, Christmas and Its Customs, 1957.
——, Easter and Its Customs, 1961.
——, English Sports and Pastimes, 1949.
——, English Shrines and Sanctuaries, 1954.
——, Saints in Folklore, 1965.
HONE, W., The Everyday Book, 1826.
——, The Table Book, 1827.
——, The Year Book, 1829.
HOPE, R. C., The Legendary Lore of the Holy Wells of England, 1893.
HOWITT, W., The Rural Life of England. 2nd ed. 1840.
HULL, E., Folklore of the British Isles, 1928.

JAMES, E. O., Seasonal Feasts and Festivals, 1961.
JAMES, M. R., Suffolk and Norfolk, 1930.
JENKIN, A. HAMILTON, Cornwall and the Cornish, 1932.
JOHNSON, W., Folk Memory, 1908.

LANCASHIRE AND CHESHIRE ANTIQUARIAN SOCIETY, Transactions of.
LEICESTERSHIRE NOTES AND QUERIES.
LEATHER, E. M., The Folk-Lore of Herefordshire, 1912.
LINCOLNSHIRE NOTES AND QUERIES.
LONG, GEORGE, The Folklore Calendar, 1930.

MACQUOID, T. & K., About Yorkshire, 1883.
MILES, C. A., Christmas in Ritual and Tradition, 1912.

NEVILLE, C., A Corner of the North, 1911.
NOTES AND QUERIES.

OLIVIER, E., Moonrakings, n.d.
OPIE, IONA AND PETER, The Lore and Language of Schoolchildren, 1959.

PATON, C. I., Manx Calendar Customs, 1939.
PINE, L. G., Traditions and Customs in Modern Britain, 1967.
PLOT, DR. ROBERT, The Natural History of Oxfordshire, 1677. The Natural History of Staffordshire, 1686.
PORTEOUS, CRICHTON, The Beauty and Mystery of Well-Dressing, 1949.

SOMERSET & DORSET NOTES AND QUERIES.
STERNBERG, T., The Dialect and Folk-Lore of Northamptonshire, 1851.
STOW, JOHN, Survey of London and Westminster, 1598.
STRUTT, JOSEPH, The Sports and Pastimes of the People of England, 1801: ed. J. C. Cox, 1903.
STUBBES, PHILIP, Anatomie of Abuses, 1583.
SUFFOLK NOTES AND QUERIES.

TEBBUTT, C. F., Huntingdonshire Folklore, n.d. (Preface, 1951.)

UDALL, L. S., Dorsetshire Folklore, 1922.
URLIN, E., Festivals, Holy Days and Saints' Days, n.d.

VAUX, J. E., Church Folk Lore, 2nd ed., 1902.

WALFORD, C., Fairs, Past and Present, 1883.
WHISTLER, L., The English Festivals, 1947.
WORCESTERSHIRE NOTES AND QUERIES.
WRIGHT, A. R., AND LONES, T. E., British Calendar Customs: England. 3 Vols., 1936-9.

YORKSHIRE NOTES AND QUERIES.

# Index